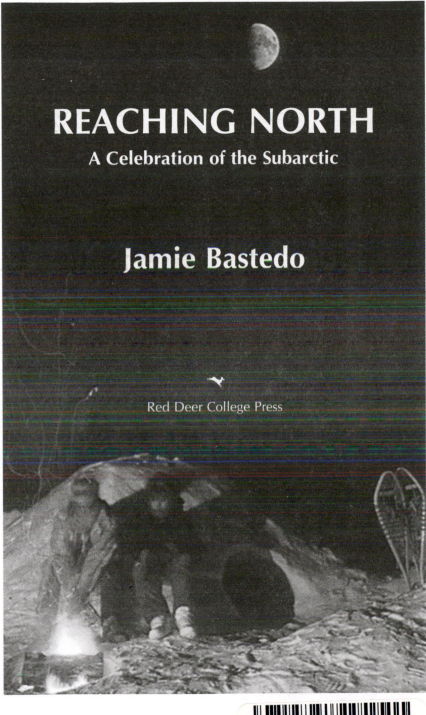

REACHING NORTH

A Celebration of the Subarctic

Jamie Bastedo

Red Deer College Press

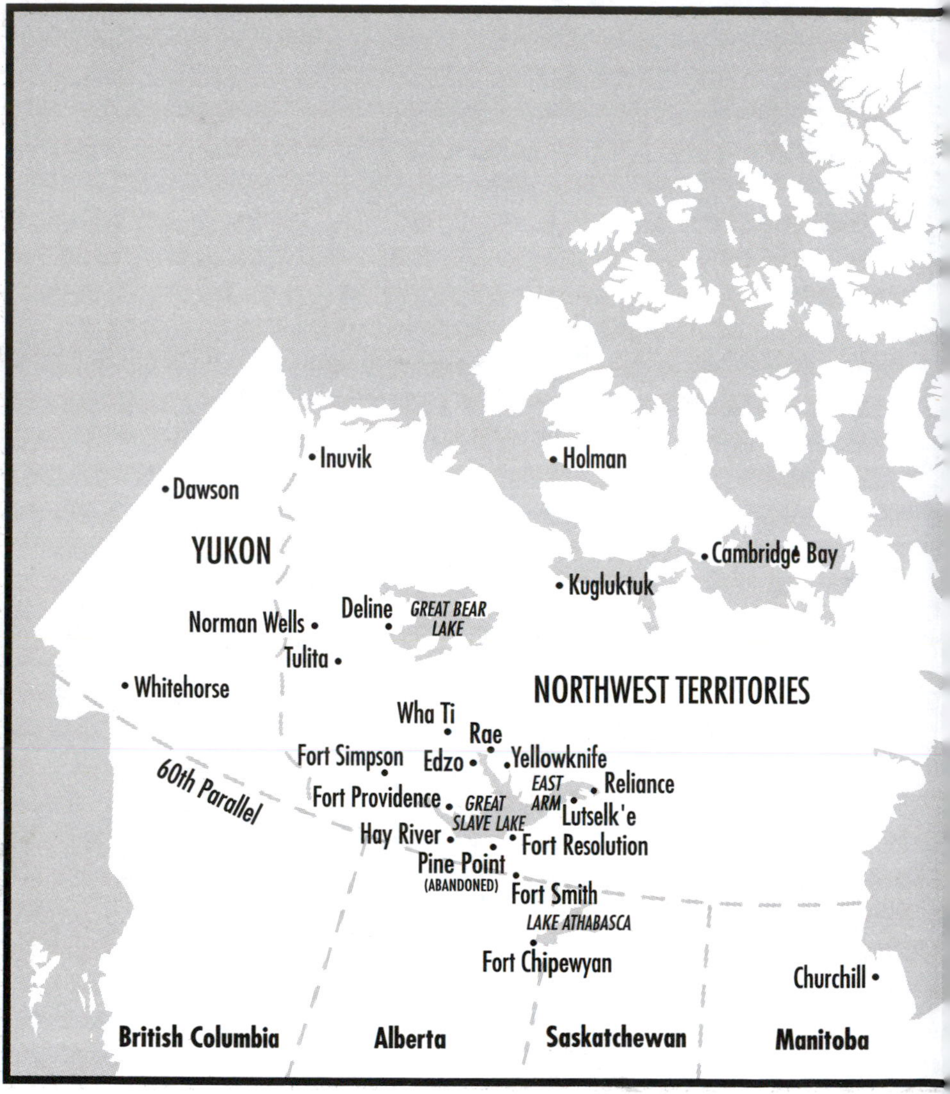

Inuvik
Holman
Dawson
YUKON
Cambridge Bay
Kugluktuk
Deline
GREAT BEAR LAKE
Norman Wells
Tulita
Whitehorse
NORTHWEST TERRITORIES
Wha Ti
Rae
Fort Simpson
Edzo
Yellowknife
60th Parallel
EAST ARM
Reliance
Fort Providence
GREAT SLAVE LAKE
Lutselk'e
Hay River
Fort Resolution
Pine Point
(ABANDONED)
Fort Smith
LAKE ATHABASCA
Fort Chipewyan
Churchill
British Columbia
Alberta
Saskatchewan
Manitoba

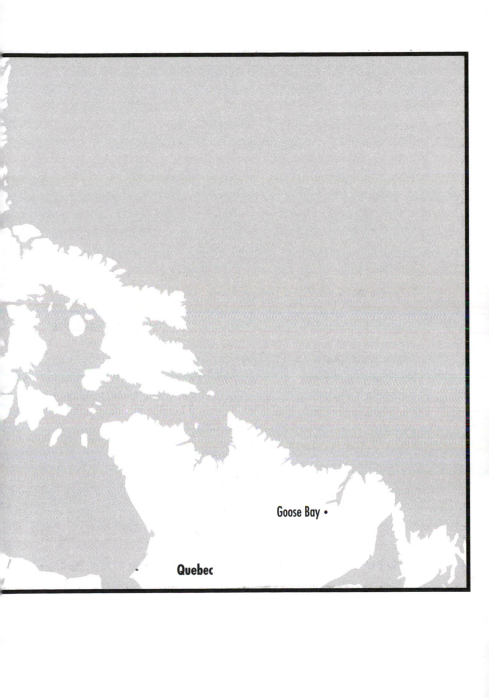

Goose Bay •

Quebec

The Publishers
Red Deer College Press
56 Avenue & 32 Street Box 5005
Red Deer Alberta Canada T4N 5H5

Acknowledgments
Cover photograph by Tessa Macintosh
Author photograph by Northern News Service
Cover design by Boldface Technologies
Text design by Dennis Johnson
Printed and bound in Canada by Webcom for
Red Deer College Press

5 4 3 2 1

Financial support provided by the Alberta Foundation for the Arts, a beneficiary of the Lottery Fund of the Government of Alberta, and by the Canada Council, the Department of Canadian Heritage and Red Deer College.

COMMITTED TO THE DEVELOPMENT OF CULTURE AND THE ARTS

THE CANADA COUNCIL | LE CONSEIL DES ARTS
FOR THE ARTS | DU CANADA
SINCE 1957 | DEPUIS 1957

For manuscript preparation the author gratefully acknowledges the financial assistance of the Canada Council and the Northwest Territories Department of Education, Culture and Employment.

Canadian Cataloguing in Publication Data
Bastedo, Jamie, 1955–
Reaching north
ISBN 0-88995-170-5
1. Canada, Northern—Description and travel. 2. Taiga ecology—Canada. 3. Natural history—Canada, Northern. I. Title.
FC3956.B37   1997   917.1904'3   C97-910529-3
F1090.5.B37   1997

For my loving wife.

*I care to live only to entice people to
look at Nature's loveliness.*
—*John Muir,* Son of the Wilderness

CONTENTS

Acknowledgments

The long process of writing this book led me in many unsuspected directions. It started life as a collection of lightly edited radio transcripts from a northern nature series I used to do regularly on CBC North. To get the manuscript to this stage in life I thank Craig Mackie, the former director of CBC North Radio, for his original inspiration.

My fledgling manuscript nestled for a while in several publishers' in-baskets until the day Dennis Johnson, Managing Editor of Red Deer College Press, picked it up and looked beyond the merry outdoor science I had presented to something much larger, much richer. "Dig deeper into these topics," he told me. "Find their real sparkle. Get personal. Get lyrical. . . . We would love to publish something like that." The manuscript metamorphosed into these stories of subarctic discovery. Thank-you, Dennis, for this prod and ongoing guidance along the way. Special thanks also to Carolyn Dearden, who helped give the book its final polish.

Now, for all those who added so much sparkle to the book's contents, here goes. Thank-you, Katsunori Nagase; may the northern lights some day tickle the sky over your Japanese home. Thank-you, Tessa Macintosh, for helping to bring Katsunori's world into mine. Thank-you, Bill Pruitt, for widening my eyes and heart to snow, and to Rick Riewe, Rosanna Strong, Richard Zieba and others for the flurry of stories about the Snowman himself. Thank-you, Steve Goff, Alan Jones and Dave Smith, for turning the geological lights on for me along (and under) the East Arm of Great Slave Lake. Thank-you, Steve Janzen, for your meticulous research on the forest fire history of the Northwest Territories and permission to adapt some of the fruits of your hard labor. Thank-you, Mike Beauregard, for your insights and tales that found their way into several chapters. Thank-you, Chris O'Brien, for being the kind of person who would hug a mosquito if you only could. And what acknowledgments have I ever written without mentioning birdman Bob Bromley, who in this book helped bring alive for me the noble character of Bill McDonald.

Among notable others who contributed to this book are Doris McCann, Joanne Bird, Bill Tait, Randy Henderson, Alan Beck, Fran Hurcomb, Nancy Buckley, Sam Bullock, Lee and Doris Smith, and R.A. MacArthur. A big thanks to all contributing photographers.

Finally, thank-you to Brenda, Jaya and Nimisha for lovingly supporting my writer's habit through those many days both thick and thin.

INTRODUCTION
REACHING NORTH

The physical landscape is baffling in its ability to transcend whatever we would make of it. It is as subtle in its expression as turns of the mind, and larger than our grasp; and yet it is still knowable.
—*Barry Lopez,* Arctic Dreams

Just weeks before his death half a century ago, the great American naturalist Aldo Leopold declared, "There are some who can live without wild things, and some who cannot." I for one put myself squarely and unabashedly in the second category. The wild thing I cannot live without is wilderness. And not a vestigial pocket of nature hemmed in on all sides by the untamed sprawl of what some call civilization, but a vast primeval wilderness to which scattered islands of human development add errant splashes of economic diversity and cultural color. And not a faraway wilderness to tug at my hopes and dreams, but one that is always immediate and near, easily accessible, never out of my peripheral vision, more or less in my face.

Where on earth then might I go to find a natural home? Scan the continents in your mind. Where are the biggest, wildest tracts of land that nature zealots like me need to stay sane? In Africa? South America? Eurasia? Three strikes. Too many people. The last thing these regions need is yet another mouth to feed. Perhaps the Australian Outback? The American Southwest? Keep swinging. Too many roads. Too little space. Remember, I have very high wilderness standards.

Next to chronic consumerism, the most widespread

trends in our present phase of human "evolution" are rampant urbanization and the plowing under of hinterlands in the name of agri-business. By default, not defiance, the greatest expanses of land as yet untouched by these trends are found where creature comforts and agricultural potential approach zero. Not surprisingly, the largest jewels to escape the ongoing looting of our planet's natural wealth are clustered around the North and South poles.

I confess that Antarctica, however huge and elemental, would be too lonely for me. When uprooting myself from my previous home in south India, I never even considered it. On the polar flip side is the Arctic, a region I often tromp over, will always be fond of, but in which I will never feather a nest. When occasionally tempted to do so, it is my unshakable affection for trees that holds me back. So by process of elimination, that leaves what? None other than the subarctic, my natural home of choice and the subject of this book.

Polar bears and icebergs, yellow poppies and jousting narwhals, half-moon ulu knives and stoneman inukshuks. Such icons of the Arctic come easily to the collective mind of North watchers everywhere, hence the deluge of coffee-table books on the subject. On the scale of a biome, the Arctic is relatively discrete and unambiguous. It can be summarily defined and instantly recognized using no more than a dozen words: "that region where the soil is permanently frozen and trees cannot grow." Less lucid are the images and words that spring to most minds when the subarctic is mentioned: the Great North Woods, muskeg and moose, bogs and bush—lots of bush. This region stretches unbroken from Labrador to Alaska and beyond, from Siberia to Scandinavia. It forms a wide evergreen crown across the North American continent. In Canada alone it covers 1.6 million square kilometers—almost the size of Mexico. And yet the subarctic is variously described as a "mental blank on the map," a "geographical blind spot" and a "rather nebulous term with a variety of definitions."

The subarctic means very different things to different people. Climatologists like to think of it as "that region in which the mean temperature exceeds 10°C for not more than four months of the year and the mean of the coldest month is not more than 0°C." Okay. Explain that to a moose. Foresters define the subarctic as "the forest–tundra transition zone plus the northern parts of the taiga or boreal forest." Still fuzzy. In the subarctic it is indeed hard to see the forest for the spruce trees because they often merge inconspicuously with tundra to the north and the dense fir forests to the south. What about ecologists? They recognize the subarctic as "that region with both forest and continuous or discontinuous permafrost." A simpler definition, yes, but the presence of permafrost is largely invisible to the untrained eye. One author of a high school textbook tried to simplify things even further, conceiving of the subarctic as "that region lying just south of the Arctic Circle (66° 30' north latitude)." This does not sound very ecological to me. Since when do biomes recognize lines of latitude? Or finally, what about the definition offered up by geographers who fancy that everything genuinely northern can be lumped into four large boxes: the Near North, Middle North, Far North and Extreme North? According to this classification, the subarctic falls neatly into the box labeled Middle North—an area bounded by lines that, on the ground, are as tangible as the Tropic of Cancer.

Can you see it yet? Neither can I. Nor, perhaps, will I ever. The entire subarctic cannot be squeezed into words any more than you can haul up a river with a fish net. Any way you look at it—through the spectacles of climate, vegetation, latitude, permafrost status or simply big lumps of land—there is something elusive about this place called the subarctic.

Instead of trying to wrestle its totality into view—as one might try to define an automobile merely in terms of concepts and mechanisms—I pin my hopes on intimacy, which brings me closer to whatever might be known as the Real Subarctic. For ultimately it is only through the lens of personal relationships that we can befriend those things that loom large and sometimes baffling in our lives. My goal in this book therefore is not to portray the quintessential nub of this oceanic wilderness. Rather it is to evoke something of its sense and spirit through one-on-one encounters.

My hope is that the stories that follow will reveal to you some of the more fascinating traits of this region's enigmatic personality. Follow the complete life cycle of a tiny snow crystal and a bedrock fault a thousand kilometers long. Enter a frozen beaver lodge in January and the heart of a midsummer fire storm. Ponder the delicate hues of a raven's egg and the riot of color discharged by a volcano of northern lights. Among your guides are a prospector, bug counter and radio broadcaster; a forest-fire ranger, deep-earth prober and ardent sky watcher; a hunter, fisherman and *courier de bois*; an ecologist, fish biologist and a few city slickers from the south. And me, an awestruck celebrant of the subarctic.

Like the six blind brothers trying for the first time to come to grips with an elephant—"It's a snake! It's a spear! It's a wall! It's a tree!"—we, your guides, serve up narrow glimpses of this land and leave its final estimation up to you. Inevitably our knowledge of this landscape (or any landscape for that matter) will always be incomplete, leaving us perpetually wanting. So it is with any relationship. But strive for intimacy, and greater knowledge will follow, always in proportion to our reach. Something I hear in the wind tells me that measured over the brief span of our lives the reaching and the grasping are the same.

KATSUNORI'S CALLING

We are very lucky people . . . to study perhaps the most beautiful natural phenomenon in the world.
—Auroral scientist Syunichi Akasofu, The Northern Lights

February 1989. The parking lot of a roadside restaurant in Hay River, Northwest Territories. A heavily built Japanese man in his midtwenties muscled a large camera bag down the narrow stairs of a northbound bus. His heart beat fast as his feet made their first contact with the frozen North. He walked stiffly toward the restaurant, then stopped suddenly as if remembering something very important. He looked up at the night sky, and for a moment the aches and worries that had been building up since leaving the bus station in Vancouver dissolved. A ghostly arm of green and yellow light spiraled above his head.

This was not the first time for Katsunori Nagase (that's *CAT-soo-nory nah-GAH-say*). He had seen the aurora borealis—or northern lights—the previous summer in Fairbanks, Alaska. He drove there from Calgary on a well-used 250cc motorcycle. Except for driving school in Japan, he had never driven on public roads anywhere on earth. But something powerful was tugging him north. "I had very poor knowledge about motorbikes and camping. I had some money, but my English level was very bad. When I ordered a hot dog, I got four cans of Coke. I got a lot of kindness and help on my travels." Remarkably he made the twenty-five-hundred-kilo-meter journey in one piece. The first question he asked when he arrived in Fairbanks was "Where is the University of Alaska?" He wanted to make face-to-face contact with some of the biggest names in auroral science, many of whom worked out of the university's Geophysical Institute. Hours and hours of reading about the northern lights had filled his head with questions, and he figured that this was the best place to get some answers. His three-year vocation as an aurora watcher began under Alaskan skies. "Yes. I saw the northern lights there," he told me. "As it was in August, even the night sky was still bright. They were not strong enough, but I felt that I would see them again."

"I've seen [the Japanese] jump around and scream and cry when they first see the lights," Bill Tait told me. Tait is president of Raven Tours, a Yellowknife-based outfitting company that helps bring Japanese tourists and the northern lights together. "Often the Japanese girls are so happy, there'll be tears streaming down their faces, freezing on their faces at forty below." Tait and his guides call themselves aurora specialists. "We get all kinds from Japan. The largest group seems to be the young lady office workers between twenty-five and forty. Then there's the silver age group, the seniors. Last are the honeymooners."

I asked Tait about the hackneyed notion that newlyweds come north hoping to conceive a child under the aurora borealis.

"That bit about bringing good luck to your kid was invented by some American television writer out of Alaska," he replied.

So why this passion to see the northern lights?

"It's not something we marketed on to them," explained Tait. "There's already a natural interest in auroras in Japan.

They had them there a hundred years ago. You see, the magnetic North Pole was farther south in those days, closer to Japan, and auroras would frequently appear in their north islands. Still, it was a real event even back then. As the magnetic North Pole migrated farther north over the years, the Japanese weren't seeing them as often. Those that did felt especially blessed. The aurora became associated with good luck. Another thing is that any natural phenomenon of such beauty is bound to appeal to the Japanese. They have such a strong aesthetic instinct."

In Inuyama City, Japan, Katsunori Nagase's family extends, under one small roof, to his parents, grandparents and elder sister. Behind the house is a tiny plot of land dedicated to home-grown rice and vegetables. When Katsunori announced his plan to give up everything to study the northern lights, his family was not pleased. "They disagreed when I went to Canada. My mother cried." This was clearly against tradition. "I was first boy. Usually first boy keeps the house and land in Japan." But the travel bug had bit Katsunori and would not let go. It fed off boyhood desires stirred by a particularly captivating TV program on the northern lights and a globetrotting high school teacher full of stories of alien lands.

Katsunori's dream took flight the day he walked away from a well-paying job as a salesman for Japanese medical supplies. The perils of taking such a leap were explained to me by a friend of his. "In Japan you dedicate yourself to the company you work with—you belong to that company. If you abandon them somewhere along the line of your career, you've had it. You take the risk of nobody else wanting to take you on. He did that."

Katsunori had made up his mind that there was more important business to attend to. "I used to go to hospitals and dealers, staying always in hotels. I worked 350 days my first year. I could get awards. As I worked hard, I had no time for myself. I could save money. But I could not throw my dream away."

Equipped with night-school English from Calgary and new insights into auroral science from Fairbanks, Katsunori felt ready to put down roots for a while in some faraway northern community.

"I decided that my next place would be a remote and very cold place. I was going to some hamlet of the Inuit. The starting point was to be Yellowknife."

Lured by the brilliant northern lights he discovered above Yellowknife and foiled by the lack of jobs farther north, he decided to stay on indefinitely. To his surprise, however, he soon discovered that this city of seventeen thousand parked smack under the auroral oval seemed to have few resources or heart for studying the northern lights.

"I asked about northern lights to Yellowknifers. But I was not satisfied. I asked tourist information about the northern lights, and they had nothing. No photos, no pictures, nothing. I thought that the person from a different place may be able to see the lights from different eyes. So I decided to take pictures myself."

The problem was that Katsunori knew next to nothing about photography let alone how to capture the fleeting northern lights on film. "My photo equipment and knowledge was poor. I did not know slide film. My camera was an electric one, the kind that freezes soon. So I studied myself from books and saved money to buy good equipment. I also got books from my sister in Japan." To finance his new camera habit, he scraped T-bone steak and arctic char bones off dishes in the kitchen of the Explorer Hotel. He mopped oil and swept gravel off the garage floor at Robinsons' Trucking.

Katsunori warms his hands while northern lights dance above his camera. (PHOTO: TESSA MACINTOSH)

With his humble savings he bought a half trashed Ford Pinto, rusty brown with badly balding tires. Now he could get out of town to get a better look at the aurora.

"He was a purist and wanted no streetlights interfering with his observations," said one of his former landlords. "He started to go out like this at least three times a week in the middle of the night."

Katsunori's viewing platform included windswept, frozen lakes, abandoned mining roads and occasionally the dented roof of his Pinto.

I once had the good fortune to watch the northern lights at play from an observation deck suspended ninety-five hundred meters above the ground. Showtime began with a loud metallic click directly above my head followed by several seconds of raspy static. The first officer's loud monotone voice jolted my mind to attention. "If you look out the right side of the plane," he said, "you'll see a good show of northern lights." Two blonde and braided heads beside me immediately glued themselves to the plastic oval window.

"Dad, look!"

I craned over for a peek between the braids. While my eyes adjusted to the night sky, all I saw were the asynchronous flashes of red beacon lights. The belly light strobed one of our jet's suspended Rolls Royce engines while the dome light briefly flooded the upper surface of the wing. My pupils gradually opened. My girls went back to their crayons. Then I saw the lights. Unseen by any terrestrially bound humans was an upside-down volcano of light dancing among the stars. A lumpy blanket of clouds twenty-five hundred meters below us glowed alternately green and pink in concert with the aurora's quivering colors. I watched the show for several minutes with my hands cupped beside both temples to block any fluorescent spillage from inside the plane. The multiple bands of light spewing from the volcano began to fold together. As they gradually merged, their radiance intensified. A mountain of light shrank to a single electrified ribbon that appeared snagged in slow motion on the razor-sharp tip of our starboard wing.

My analytically inclined left brain grappled with the spectacle before me. It posed the question: What caused this wonderful effect? I imagined a colossal solar squall ten times the size of the earth. Several days ago, it hurled aloft a tornado of fire that rose a hundred thousand kilometers above the sun's raging surface. A mass of highly charged electrons and protons broke loose from the storm and was jettisoned into deep space. Call it solar wind. Ionized plasma. Electrostatic Jell-O. It blasted toward us at a hundred kilometers per second. Twenty-four hours ago it fell within the purview of our planet. Three minutes back, or about sixty-five thousand kilometers away, the earth's magnetic field mercifully deflected the solar wind—without this protection it would have killed us all. As a large boulder intercedes in the flow of white water, our magnetic field bent the solar wind into a teardrop-shaped torrent of charged particles that streamed past the planet. On their way by, some particles were dragged down by powerful magnetic tentacles rooted near the earth's poles. At around one thousand kilometers up, the blazing began. The solar wind slammed into atmospheric gases, exciting them, energizing them, igniting them into an auroral display of ionospheric neon. Hydrogen, nitrogen and oxygen glowed red, violet and green. Or they might as easily have glowed green, blue and yellow-green respectively, depending on the collision altitude, the atmospheric temperature, the amount of energy released, and so on and so on. . . . I blinked hard.

Never before had I seen the northern lights from this angle or altitude. Nor had I ever seen the peculiar flashes of white light that now peppered my view of the sky. They were becoming more frequent, fully illuminating the wing with each flash. Was our tail on fire? My left brain gave up the struggle. My aesthetically inclined right brain sat up and took notice. Outside my plane window, the lights danced. Cosmic choreography. That was enough: the lights danced.

I suddenly pulled back from the window and glanced up and down the aisle. No less than twenty-five Japanese tourists had their Pentaxes, Minoltas and Canons pressed against the plastic, frantically trying to document their first tryst with the northern lights. So many of them had lurched over to my side that had our plane been any smaller I felt sure that it might develop a disturbing starboard list.

Bill Tait explained to me why Yellowknife is a tourist magnet for Japanese aurora hunters. "Inuvik's too far north. Fairbanks is good, but they get a lot of maritime weather with lots of fronts going through from the Pacific. Yellowknife is nicely placed under the aurora oval, which stretches all the way from Fairbanks down to Churchill."

The auroral oval is a concentrated zone of intense geomagnetic activity that hovers above the earth like a thirteen-thousand-kilometer-wide doughnut parked at around sixty to seventy degrees latitude. It sucks the solar wind, concentrating its energy, steering it close to the earth. Within the north and south ovals—*auroral glories* as they were once called—atmospheric collisions and hence electrostatic colors reach their peak. Theoretically a person in Yellowknife could watch the sky all night, every night, and with good weather see northern lights 243 times a year, or about three nights out of five. Sky watchers in Churchill, Manitoba, could expect to see them 190 times, or about every other night. The numbers drop quickly as you go south: Edmonton, 90; Winnipeg, 75; Ottawa, 35. Torontonians should consider themselves lucky to see the northern lights at all, since the very best they could expect is 18 shows a year.

"We also get lots of high-pressure clear skies," continued Tait, "so we stand a good chance of seeing them when they're happening." In the orientation package given to his Japanese guests, Tait includes a printout of local weather data on cloud

Japanese aurora hunters bundled for a sled dog ride while waiting for night to fall over Yellowknife. (PHOTO: FRAN HURCOMB)

cover anticipated throughout the year. During the peak visitation months, January through March, Tait is happy to point out that the odds of perfectly clear skies are over 40 percent. "Plus we have good airline services and hotels. It's still pretty spooky for the Japanese to come to such a remote little place. All this adds up to a good little adventure."

Tourists who sign up for Tait's Great Canadian Experience can fish through a meter of lake ice for Great Northern Pike, enjoy caribou sausage, glazed baby carrots and hot peaches in a cozy log cabin thirty kilometers out of town, slide down a bedrock hill on sealskin toboggans, visit an igloo and go trekking through the boreal bush on snowshoes. Other packages offer dog sledding, snowmobiling and caribou viewing. But for the Japanese these are all sideshows to the night's big event: the Aurora Watch. Dressed in rented red parkas they travel to carefully selected pilgrimage sites on a minibus that takes them down a deserted ice road, or behind panting sled dogs that carry them giggling out to the center of a frozen lake, or by a torchlit walk through the woods to an elevated observation deck especially designed for auroral viewing.

"We have an 80 percent success rate for seeing the northern lights," said one of Tait's guides, "and that makes everybody happy. We had twenty-three people from other countries out on the ice the other night, looking at the northern lights. Sure enough the aurora came, and a corona happened right above our heads. The Germans, the British, they got pretty excited. But it wasn't something that would drive them to come here. Not the way it does the Japanese."

The average North of Sixty adventure for Japanese tourists lasts two and a half days. Occasionally they stay three days. The more persistent aurora watchers will stay four, maybe even five days. Any vigil longer than this would be most peculiar. Katsunori stayed almost three years.

While living under Yellowknife skies, Katsunori enjoyed a front-row seat in one of the most promising auroral theaters on earth. But the call of the far North continued to tug at him. By the dead of his first winter he had squirreled away enough dollars to think seriously about such a trip. He decided that the farthest north he could afford to fly was Holman, his "hamlet of the Inuit," located at 70°44' north latitude on the west side of Victoria Island. He arrived there just before the darkest day of the year. The sun had not shone on the 326 people of Holman since the end of November. His hope was to see what the aurora looked like during what most people call the daytime.

"I went to Holman as I wanted to take photos of the afternoon northern lights. I saw them at 3:00 P.M. But the sky was still bright on the horizon of the south. My purpose was failed."

Though it was true, as one friend said, that "anything he

did was motivated to see the lights," Katsunori took a sort of holiday up there in Holman, turning his attention from the dim high latitude auroras to the new people around him. "I spent a good time there for three weeks during Christmas and New Years. I was fine. My original plan was for two weeks. The first delay was an airplane problem. Second was a punctured tire at the relay station and no extra tire. Third was seven seats only on the plane, but we were eight passengers including sick people. As I was the eighth person, I waited seven days for the next one. I phoned my manager. When I came back to Yellowknife, I was fired."

Self-reliance came naturally to Katsunori, says Mike Beauregard, a hard-rock geologist who came to know him through a kindred interest in unusual earthly phenomena. "He wasn't about to get into a position where he had to be responsible to anyone," says Mike. The nature of Katsunori's peculiar calling and his itinerant status placed him on the outer fringes of mainstream northern society. He waited and watched and photographed mostly alone, mostly late at night. But his cherished independence took a temporary back seat to his team spirit whenever he stepped onto the soccer pitch or gym floor. According to Mike, "he had exceptional feet and knew how to use 'em. All of a sudden everyone's jaws would drop, and there was Kats popping out of the sidelines with the ball."

Katsunori allowed himself the passion of soccer but rarely strayed far from his first love, even after an exhausting game. "He'd get me out of bed at 4:00 A.M. to tell me about 'a really good one,'" says Mike, who occasionally joined him for some night-stalking adventures. When most of the town was headed for bed, Katsunori might pull up uninvited in front of Mike's basement apartment window and lean on his Pinto's horn. "Move over. I'll drive," Mike would say, having concluded that this was the safer option. "Kats was a bloody grandmother of a driver. Too damned cautious," says Mike. "He'd crawl along those dark roads, sometimes right into the ditch. One night he got three flat tires in a row." It seemed to Mike that behind the wheel, Katsunori was either looking at the northern lights or looking for a good place to view the northern lights. "He would have killed for a good hill around town!"

Katsunori probably owes his life to that Pinto's heater, which worked overtime throughout his many roadside stops. Again and again, out of the hatchback door, came the tripod, the camera bag and, if he remembered, a thermos of hot tea. "His camera was always pointed at the sky," Mike told me. "He paid little attention to the foreground. It was the lights that mattered. Always the lights."

The aurora's final waning or the inescapable need for sleep signaled the end of a long night's vigil for Katsunori. He would reluctantly pack up, then turn down a snow-packed road that led to the garish lights of town. Time to head home, which, for the last six months of his northern sojourn, was the Blue Raven Guest House.

"I said 'room with a view' and he went for it," said owner Tessa Macintosh. Finding Tessa was a lucky strike for Katsunori. Not only was her house perched high and alone on a bald promontory of Precambrian rock that offered an unbroken view of the southern sky—his favorite quadrant—but Tessa was a photographer, a professional with a fondness for northern lights.

Once Katsunori got settled, Tessa let a respectful few days pass before she gave in to her curiosity about his love of the lights. "I tried to see if he had some sort of mystical sense about the aurora, to see whether it was a romantic inclination or something that brought him here. It wasn't. He would deny this. He was a very scientific, practical guy." Tessa once tried to dig deeper. "What is it, what *is* it?" she asked him.

"It's just fascinating and I want to study it," replied Katsunori.

"He wanted to learn everything he could about them," said Tessa. "He had to do it. He couldn't help himself. His enthusiasm was incredible."

Katsunori brought some of that enthusiasm to bear on Tessa's brain. He politely scavenged from her any tips and tricks that would help train his camera to see the northern lights exactly as his eyes did. "He wasn't really much of a photographer when he got here. But he certainly became a good one over time," said Tessa. "It gets easier with practice. The lights go quickly astray, then disappear. Like any natural phenomenon, it requires a lot of patience to get a good shot. And it's often in very cold weather."

Next to camera equipment Katsunori gave high priority to premium outdoor clothes, including a fur-trimmed, goose-down parka, heavy mitts and minus-forty-degree snow boots—anything to keep the cold at bay and prolong his night watches, which sometimes stretched beyond eight hours. And that was *starting* usually after 9:00 P.M. He knew there was little point in going earlier. With a straight face he once told Tessa, "There's a ten o'clock showing and a twelve o'clock showing and a two o'clock showing—just like the movies." Katsunori's favorite? Midnight.

"Usually midnight one is better than evening and morning one. This is the general pattern. Some travel agency took tourists to go out and see northern lights between nine o'clock and twelve o'clock. It is too early to see good one usually. The tourists saw evening one. Good northern lights danced in the sky when they were in their beds."

Katsunori not only developed an uncanny knack for predicting curtain time for the lights. He also became very good at predicting their intensity, thanks to nightly calls to a data bank in Boulder, Colorado. From the day he moved in, Tessa's phone bills became spotted with fifty-eight-second calls to the U.S. Space Environment Sciences Center—an electronic clearinghouse of earthly and interplanetary information.

"Every night he'd he'd sit there in our little wooden school desk listening to a recording that gave the latest information on the sun's activity," said Tessa. "So he always knew when to expect the best lights." Katsunori explained, "The information is on a tape message. They give a number for solar flux, the A-index, and a number for the strength of the geomagnetic field, the K-index. They also forecast the geomagnetic field for the next twenty-four hours. I need all this. If the two indexes are high and the forecast is good, then it will be good for northern lights."

The equation appears simple. Add together lots of solar plasma pointed our way with a strong geomagnetic catcher's mitt around the earth, and you're probably in for a good light show. But Katsunori was familiar with the fallibility of science. "According to the manager in Boulder, their forecast can be 90 percent wrong. The forecast is still okay because they have the experience of long years. If they have no experience I do not believe them. Anyhow, for me, the information is still very valuable. Better than nothing. Do not believe the information all the time. Even the forecast of weather is wrong sometimes, you know. Same as this."

"Kats was a pro," according to one acquaintance, "but also terribly modest." He was in the northern lights business for neither fame nor money.

"This will be nothing," he once confided to Tessa, harking back to his lack of formal training in either photography or auroral science. "It's useless," he would say in gloomier moods. Yet, the next moment, he would wheel his unwilling Pinto down the driveway, then head off again under the stars to the wilderness fringe of town.

After thousands of photos and about as many phone calls, the fruits of Katsunori's labor began to ripen. "After a while I was asked about my photos by the museum, the government of Northwest Territories, a publisher in Ontario, the Canadian Embassy in Tokyo and many Japanese travel agencies. A big photo agency in Japan, TV shows and magazines also got interested." His impeccable images convinced the editors of *Equinox*, *Up Here* and *Astronomy* to feature his photos, some of which made the front cover. Other requests came from the University of Alberta, the University of Alaska in Fairbanks and several southern art galleries. Katsunori's humble enthusiasm for the northern lights infected radio listeners around the world during an interview on Radio Canada International. His photos soon decorated northern travel brochures meant to lure upwardly mobile Japanese to Canada's North.

One phone call to his media contacts in Japan led to the delivery of an entire TV crew to Yellowknife to film a documentary on the northern lights. As project coordinator, Katsunori helped his avid guests plan their assault on the lights and generally made them feel at home during their brief stay. He also helped arrange for an aircraft charter because of all the cloudy weather they were getting. The film crew's first and last glimpse of the northern lights was snatched above the clouds. "Maybe they come back again," he reflected as they toted their precious film back to Japan.

"Wherever he ends up," said one feature article on Katsunori, "he can lay claim to one of the most unique photographic portfolios in the world. Although he downplays his accomplishment, he says it did take a lot of practice." Practice, single-minded dedication and a liberal allowance of time and patience. These he had. The article concluded that "he is perhaps the only photographer in North America to make a living from the northern lights."

March 23, 1991. 6:15 P.M. As he had hundreds of times before, Katsunori got up from the supper table and immediately reached for the phone. The numbers fed to him from a tape machine in Boulder told him that something big was going to happen that night.

"The A-index for the night was very high. I never heard it like this. But I expected something interesting near the equinox. Good northern lights after sunspot peaks." From "new books" Katsunori had learned that the best auroral displays often occur during the week before and after the spring and fall equinoxes. "I could not imagine what kind of northern lights might appear. The information was very high. It was coming. Something very good I have never seen." His pulse raced. "When I heard from the telephone very high A-index, my heart was beating with much excitement, even the blood vessels of my brain." After fifty-eight seconds, he swung the phone back into its cradle and turned automatically towards the expansive south-facing windows of the Blue Raven Guest House. Waiting for Katsunori was a perfectly still, blue-black sky. He saw no trace of lights, not even a glimmer, but it was still early. Though he had no idea what was coming, he knew more or less when it would arrive.

Three hours later and five degrees to the north, people in Kugluktuk up on the Arctic coast began phoning down to their friends in Yellowknife, concerned that they were seeing some kind of distant apocalypse. "What's going on down there?" they asked while looking out their windows at an eerie red glow on the southern horizon. That same night, in the community of Wha Ti on Lac La Martre, an adolescent

Dogrib girl came in from the cold and asked a visiting dog musher, "Did you see the red sky? Jesus is coming."

9:30 P.M. Waltzing three hundred kilometers above Katsunori's smiling, fur-trimmed face was an intense rose-colored curtain draped across a moon-washed sky. It moved slowly, ponderously, as if weighed down by the richness of its color and magnitude of its light. I asked Katsunori how he felt that night out on the lake ice. "I did not dance. I did not shout anything. When I saw the red one, my body was shaking." But there was work to be done. He turned to the challenge of trapping this extraordinary light on celluloid. He dropped to his knees, unzipped his bulky camera bag and flicked on his penlight. Its beam came to rest on a F2.8 15 mm fisheye lens. While holding his steamy breath, he mated the lens with a Canon F-1 body and clicked it home. He took aim at his beloved aurora. With the drifted lake surface bowed like a soup dish and the camera tilted skyward at about forty-five degrees, this unusually cooperative cloud of color fit neatly into his lens. He opened the aperture wide and turned the focus ring to infinity. Click. For seven seconds, the first frame of his Fujichrome 800 ASA film was bathed in ethereal red light. Click. Ten seconds. Click. Twelve seconds. Click. Fifteen. Then he closed down the lens by a couple stops and started all over. Click. Seven seconds. Click. Ten. Click. After bracketing dozens of frames at different exposures he paused to stomp his chilled feet and gaze up with naked eyes at the rarest of auroras. What went through his mind at that moment is hard for him to say.

"I might be in their reverence," he recalled. "I might have said, 'I got it. I finally got it.'"

Early the next morning Katsunori was back on the phone again. First he called his soccer coach. "Yes, the night of red one. My soccer team captain was working at the airport that night. He got a phone call from a lady who said there was a forest fire over there. That was red northern lights. He also told me when he talked to a pilot. The pilot said, 'Even the ground was red. The snow was reflecting the lights.'" Then Katsunori phoned the fire department. "I wanted to see if they got lots of calls that night. Yes, lots of people phoned to the fire department saying, 'Forest fire!'" In 1938 a similar show of red aurora over the northeastern Atlantic convinced the British populace that Windsor Castle was on fire.

"I remember that night," Tessa Macintosh told me. "Mike and I had just come home from a dance and found Kats sitting there in the dark. All he could say was, 'Unbelievable. *Unbelievable!* Very, very unusual. Red aurora!' He was so excited to see it just before he had to leave the North, after studying the lights for over two years."

When he picked up his pictures of the red aurora a few days before leaving town, Katsunori was a happy man. "He was very particular about getting the correct color," recalled Tessa. "Very fussy. Sometimes he would show me a picture and say, 'No. That's no good! That's wrong color.'" When he proudly showed Tessa his favorite picture of the red aurora, a crimson, rabbit-shaped cloud wearing the moon for a tail, she said, "It wasn't *that* red was it?" Katsunori smiled and said, "Exactly. Yes!"

It was time to go. On Katsunori's way through security at the Vancouver airport, a customs agent stopped him briefly to explain the ropes of staying on in Canada—for good if he wanted to. "The immigrant office man said to me, 'You could apply as an immigrant since you spent almost three years here. Time to go back to Japan if you want to work here again. So think about it.' I felt that it was a good time to go home and think about my future. So I decided to find a job in Japan. I could not travel anymore to lots of countries, but

I was fine with that. I got good friends in Yellowknife and Holman. This was over."

Six years after Katsunori took up the spade once again to work a small plot of land in Inuyama City, after winning back his mother with his dazzling photos published in magazines and broadcast on TV, after landing a steady tourism job at a state park hotel—"I can take vacation when I want to"—and after a brief honeymoon back in Holman of all places, Katsunori hears my voice among many wondering why he did it.

"Why? Because I am Japanese. This is not enough answer for you, is it? The question is a most difficult one for me to explain except for Japanese. If you know about Japanese very well, you do not have to ask me." Without really answering my question, Katsunori politely turned away my desire to probe any deeper. Somewhere in his passion and his pictures lies the answer.

SNOW SAGA

Snow, the beautiful snow . . . It not only quickens that response to the dainty and the exquisite that makes us human, but equally arouses our desire to understand, our curiosity to know, the how and the why of this purest gem of surpassing beauty and of a myriad, myriad forms. —W. J. Humphreys, glaciologist, 1931

Defying gravity, a microscopic fleck of volcanic ash sailed freely twelve kilometers above a sawtooth chain of limestone peaks. Ten weeks had passed since its ejection from the bowels of a Filipino volcano on the other side of the planet. The upper atmosphere was relatively calm this full moon night in November, and temperatures had stabilized at minus twenty-five degrees Celsius. All around but not touching the fleck of ash were invisible molecules of water vapor, oscillating randomly through space, free from one another's attraction.

Moisture levels in the air rose gradually through the night as warm westerly surface winds swept over the snowy mountain peaks and sent more water vapor aloft. The upper atmosphere gradually became supersaturated with vapor. The inevitable collision occurred just before dawn as the moon sank towards the horizon. A lone molecule of water bumped into the ash fleck and instantly condensed into a seed crystal of solid ice. One by one other molecules of water vapor were magnetically pulled toward the crystal and fused to its rapidly growing skeleton. Within each molecule two small hydrogens aligned themselves around a larger oxygen much like

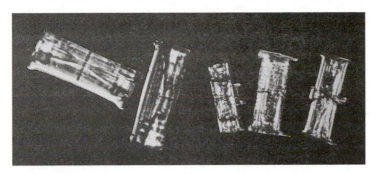

Column crystals, a key ingredient in the making of sun dogs.
(PHOTO: WILSON BENTLEY)

the ears on a Mickey Mouse hat. Each hydrogen atom stuck out at an angle of 120 degrees, giving the growing crystal a six-sided symmetry that echoed the molecular shape of water.

Within two hours the crystal encasing the ash fleck had increased its size a thousandfold. Like the tens of billions of snow crystals now hovering nearby, it had assumed the shape of a perfect hexagonal shaft. Together these pencil-shaped columns of ice drew a thin milky sheet of cirrostratus clouds across the eastern sky. When rays from the rising sun shone through the clouds, they broke into a wide halo of orange and green light: a sun dog.

Far to the west, in the foothills of the Mackenzie Mountains, a native trapper emerged from his log cabin to gather firewood for his stove. While reaching for a birch log high up on his woodpile, he happened to glance up at the brilliant ring around the sun. He remembered how his grandfather had told him that a sun dog meant that the sun was pulling its parka ruff up around its face. "It's going to snow soon for sure," his grandfather would say whenever he saw that ring of light.

Twenty-seven hundred kilometers to the east and south is the University of Manitoba, main base came of Dr. Bill Pruitt. On campus they call him the Snowman or Dr. Snow or simply, but not without respect, that snow guy. Even without knowing anything about him, one might see Pruitt strolling easily through the halls of the zoology building and conclude from his appearance alone that he hailed from some far northern land of snow and ice. The North Pole perhaps. His stout form, long whitish-gray beard, ruddy complexion, proudly bald head and quizzical eyes rimmed with smile lines suggest forcibly the image of an elf, if not Santa himself, disguised as a professor.

Man of snow, man of science. Both distinctions come easily to Pruitt. Early in his probationary period at the University of Manitoba, he gave a bracing talk on the dynamics of what he called the arctic heat sink and its central role in wreaking cold temperatures on much of the country. During the applause that followed, the head of the department of zoology, Dr. Harold Welch, turned excitedly to one of his colleagues and announced, "We've just *got* to get this chap. He's the spitting image of Charles Darwin."

By reputation Pruitt is what some would call a glaciologist, a snow scientist. Theoretically this somewhat obscure body of knowledge includes not only the study of snow on the ground but also snow and ice in the atmosphere, ice on lakes, rivers and the sea, ground ice and glaciers; and ice on other planets and in outer space. Glaciology is in short the study of frozen water anywhere it exists in any of its virtually infinite forms. While no doubt fascinated by all this, Pruitt is, after all, a zoologist, and his particular passion is to explore the ecological links between snow and the animals that live on it or in it. And since snow is, as he says, "the quintessential northern material," it is no surprise that his studies of

Bill Pruitt blends work and play during a 1967 ski trip through Newfoundland's Gros Morne National Park. (PHOTO: RICK RIEWE)

snow ecology drew him ever northward to the boreal forest, where winter directs the ebb and flow of life for well over half the year. After a fifty-year quest grappling with the riddles posed by snow, the passion endures. "As time goes on," says Pruitt, "and I learn more and more about how snow affects animals, I become even *more* interested in it."

Pruitt has a rather unique but eminently logical way of looking at snow. In structural terms he puts snow on equal footing with lead, zinc, gold or any other commonly understood mineral. If a mineral is a "naturally occurring inorganic element having an orderly internal structure and characteristic composition, crystal form and physical properties," then who could possibly argue with Pruitt? The only qualifier he adds is that snow comes and goes somewhat more quickly than other minerals. A "periodic mineral" is what he calls it. A snow crystal falling through the air is a "hydrometeor" to Pruitt for that indeed is what it is: a chunk of frozen water flying through space. Furthermore Pruitt will go out of his way to tell you that a snow *crystal* should never be confused with a snow*flake*, which technically speaking is "an assemblage of individual snow crystals which have collided and remained glued together during their fall through the atmosphere." And he asks you to visualize snow on the ground in its virgin undisturbed state as nothing more or less than "an emulsion of air and ice" with the better part—most of it actually—being just air. All this is simply common sense to Pruitt.

His unusual notions about snow can be grasped by anyone willing to take a good look at it, whether or not they have a string of legitimizing degrees. Unlike the relatively inaccessible worlds of physics, chemistry and other orthodox sciences, the world of snow is for most North Americans as handy as a step beyond the back porch in January. Over half the northern hemisphere is covered in snow for part of the year. Yet to some members of the scientific community and the funding bodies that feed it, there seems to be something quaintly eccentric, almost suspect, about wanting to seriously study a substance as ubiquitous as snow. As a result one of Pruitt's chronic frustrations is that when seeking research money, he usually has to piggyback his snow studies on other more reputable subjects. Quoting Voltaire, he complains that, "here we have a country of *quelques arpents de neige*"—nothing but snow—"but very little is known about how animals and plants are affected by its characteristics." Why is there such mass illiteracy and sanctioned prejudice regarding snow? To this day Pruitt still can't figure it out. The situation seems to him as baffling as it is absurd.

The column-shaped snow crystal continued to lengthen molecule by molecule until it became too heavy for the wan-

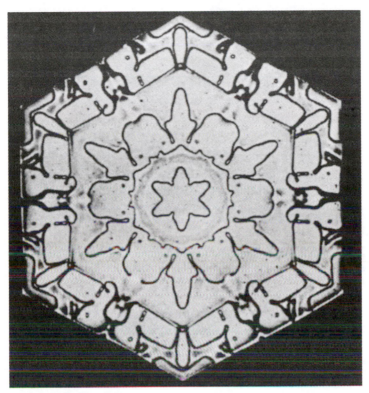

Hexagonal plate. (PHOTO: WILSON BENTLEY)

ing air currents and faint updrafts to keep it aloft. It started to fall towards the mountains far below. Just before leaving the ice cloud, it collided with two other crystals: perfect six-sided plates that glued themselves to each end of the column. As a whole the crystal now looked like a free-falling Roman pillar, complete with pedestal and lintel attached. The capped column drifted slowly through uniform atmospheric conditions until it crossed an abrupt threshold eight kilometers above the earth. At this elevation the air suddenly became much wetter and more turbulent. Swirling convection cur-

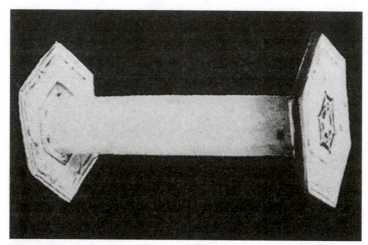

Column crystal capped with hexagonal plates. (PHOTO: WILSON BENTLEY)

rents sent the crystal tumbling rapidly end over end. One plate disintegrated into splinters of ice. Part of the other plate tore free and sailed off into the night. The rigid column structure endured in spite of strong mechanical stresses created by the wind.

Moments later the spinning half-capped crystal penetrated a water cloud composed of supercooled droplets held in fragile suspension fifteen degrees below the temperature at which water normally freezes. The end of the crystal with the broken plate acted as a kind of magnetic screen, attracting water droplets that froze instantly into tiny uneven granules of rime. As more ice built up on one end, the crystal gradually stopped tumbling and dropped, rimed-side down, through the cloud and into the clear mountain air below.

Four kilometers from the ground, the column crystal crashed into a large six-armed stellar crystal that was falling at a much slower rate. The two interlocked crystals descended

A stellar crystal: miracle in ice. (PHOTO: WILSON BENTLEY)

steadily for another three kilometers. Surface winds increased dramatically beyond this point, and the crystals were swept sideways for a few minutes, then suddenly upward, all the way back into the water cloud. The resulting wind stress and heavy riming took a toll on the stellar crystal, which was reduced to a two-armed ice-encrusted vestige of its former splendor. The attached column retained most of its structural integrity, although it too was heavily coated with grains of rime during repeated journeys in and out of the water cloud.

When the crystal finally settled to earth thirty minutes later, only the rigid column structure remained. The stellar fragment had been knocked off during a collision with a hailstone. What was left of the attached plate had become so thick with frozen rime that it snapped off from centrifugal forces alone, leaving one end of the column with a jagged irregular edge. Still encased inside the column remnant was the ash nucleus around which the original crystal had formed. Near the Yukon–Northwest Territories border, this primal alliance of ash and ice now rested on a steep south-facing slope below a fish-tailed peak with no name.

It had taken three hours for the snow crystal to make the twelve kilometer journey to this spot. The clouds that spawned and shaped the crystal were now largely spent. The amphitheater of fresh-fallen snow glowed faintly blue as the moon regained its prominence in the night sky.

Bill Pruitt grew up on a farm in northern Virginia. One lasting memento of this chapter of his life is a deep-seated aversion to eating chicken or duck or any fowl for that matter. They're "all foul" to him. One colleague attributes this to "too many hours in the hen house shoveling chicken shit." Was this the subliminal training ground for his lifelong fascination for animal scats? Not likely. Whenever he could, Pruitt would escape to the fresh air and freedom of the mixed woods near his farm. "I was not a good farm boy," he admits. "I used to slip away at every opportunity to spend time in the woods looking at critters and plants." Snow was only a minor player on his outdoor stage in those days. In Virginia you were lucky if any decent snow stayed more than four weeks a year, if at all. But the north country already was tugging on the imagination of young Bill Pruitt, calling to him sweetly through the writings and paintings of American naturalist

Ernest Thompson Seton. "My greatest inspirations were *Rolf in the Woods, Two Little Savages, The Library of Woodcraft, Wild Animals I Have Known*, and a host of others. I might add that virtually every field biologist of my generation got their early interest from Seton."

To this day Pruitt keeps Seton's memory tangibly close to his heart in the form of a caribou toe bone that hangs on his chest from a silver chain. While studying caribou along the shore of Artillery Lake in the Northwest Territories, Pruitt discovered a primitive campsite that exactly fit the description of one visited by Seton half a century earlier. In Seton's published diary, well thumbed by Pruitt, he told how his native guide had shot a caribou passing through camp. Pruitt found a caribou toe bone at that very spot and has treasured it ever since. Why?

"Because, who knows," he muses, "maybe Seton himself ate the rest."

It was not until the late 1940s, when Pruitt started a PhD at the University of Michigan, that he locked on to snow as a focus for his research. It happened during the course of his field work at Douglas Lake in the wilds of northern Michigan. "My subject was an investigation of the physical factors that influenced the local distribution of *Blarina*, the short-tailed shrew," remembers Pruitt. "I set up a series of study areas, one acre each, in vegetation types from a very fresh burn to old-growth beech, maple, hemlock forest. I exhaustively trapped each area in order to determine the population of *Blarina* in each. I had homemade sensors for soil temperature and moisture on each plot." Pruitt is as resourceful as he is thorough. Over the course of several months he took thousands of measurements, recording all the physical aspects that he could think of to monitor changes in the shrew's tiny world, its microhabitat.

To his surprise it was only after the snow started flying that he was able to wrest some sense out of the data and identify the key variable influencing the distribution of shrews. "As the seasons progressed it became clear that the plots with the most snow cover had the most equitable habitat conditions for *Blarina*." Pruitt was on to something.

After receiving his doctorate in zoology in 1952, Pruitt carried his hunches about snow into a postdoctoral fellowship. After all, he said, "that year there were absolutely no jobs in vertebrate zoology," so why not carry on with field work, his favorite pastime? This time he set up his traps farther south on a University of Michigan reserve near Ann Arbor. "Here I repeated the field work I had done in northern Michigan, but in quite a different environment with very little snow cover, most of which was ephemeral." Pruitt discovered that the shrews of this region chose their microhabitats "with considerably more rigor" than those under the longer-lasting snow of northern Michigan. "This *really* tweaked my interest, and I suppose my decision to study the effects of snow cover on mammals began."

Pruitt embarked on a research path down which very few had trod. He soon discovered that those who went before him left scanty signs of their passage: a few obscure papers and monographs, most of which were unintelligible to Pruitt because he didn't read Russian or Finnish or Norwegian. As luck or fate would have it, Pruitt met a Dr. William Prydchodko in 1953, a zoologist who had just emigrated from Ukraine. He told Pruitt about an exciting book on the ecology of snow by one of his comrades, A.N. Formozov, written, of course, in Russian. That did it. Pruitt resolved on the spot to learn Russian so he could have access to this critical work.

"Over the next few years I struggled with the language.

Bill Prydchodko and I laboriously translated the book, sending paragraphs and chapters back and forth in Russian, German and garbled English. After a number of years we finished it." Thanks to the commitment of another zoologist and friend, Dr. Bill Fuller at the University of Alberta, the book was finally published. Pruitt happily reports that "it went through two printings and has been of exceptional value to northern biologists."

More field work looked pretty good to Pruitt after such a project, and luckily the job market for zoologists was beginning to thaw. Breakup came when a private laboratory in Fairbanks, Alaska, made him a tempting offer. They wanted him to study small mammal distributions and factors influencing their survival. He gleefully took the job and was soon out setting and checking his traps and coaxing secrets from the subarctic snow. Another plumb job came along in 1957, when the Canadian Wildlife Service hired Pruitt to track caribou as they wandered across northern Manitoba, Saskatchewan and the Northwest Territories. With his wife, Erna, and young baby, he literally followed the herd for an entire year, sometimes by airplane, occasionally by canoe, most often by dog team over the snow.

"Bill Pruitt did arctic field biology like nobody had ever done it before," said Dr. Brina Kessel, the woman who snapped up Pruitt soon after he returned to civilization. She headed the biology department at the University of Alaska and hired him as an associate professor and field research coordinator. It was during Pruitt's time in Alaska that he picked a fight with what one colleague called "the most evil man in recent American history," Dr. Edward Teller.

Unlike the job market, the Cold War was experiencing anything but a thaw and had reached its icy fingers into the farthest corners of the state. Dr. Teller, the nuclear physicist who sired the hydrogen bomb, was fond of testing his invention in what he referred to as the "coastal wastelands" of Alaska. Pruitt's field studies, besides documenting the dependency of many northern mammals on snow, pointed to, as he stated, "a woeful lack of knowledge" about the effects of radioactive fallout on arctic animals and plants.

Pruitt and three other field biologists known as The Gang of Four made their concerns widely known among both scientists and the public. Opposition to further nuclear testing in Alaska mounted. Teller and the Atomic Energy Commission (AEC) pressed on, deciding it was time to demonstrate a peaceful use of H-bombs by blowing a chunk out of the Alaskan shoreline to create an artificial harbor. The plan was labeled Project Chariot and called for the detonation of up to six thermonuclear bombs. Pruitt turned up the volume of his campaign by an order of magnitude. The AEC set blast time for March or April, when, according to one press release, "most small mammals and plants are under snow-cover." The public was told not to worry, that snow would provide a safe radiation shield over the land during the blast. Then all would be rinsed clean by the spring melt. Pruitt and his gang took particular exception to the commission's unfounded notions about snow, citing the popular misconception that the Arctic is completely snow-covered all winter. They advised the AEC that snow-cover at the proposed blast site was "very sparse" due to high coastal winds. They noted that some of the botanist's study plots had been "70 percent bare of snow" and that most plants would lie naked and exposed to radiation at blast time.

This business about snow was not well received by Teller's and Pruitt's superiors. Discussion of possible radiation effects was judged "not pertinent" to the biological research undertaken by the university, most of which in those days was being paid for by the AEC. The FBI opened files on Pruitt and other "dissenting professors." These files got fairly thick before the fight was over. In the end Teller did not get his harbor, thanks largely to Pruitt, and Pruitt did not get his tenure, thanks largely to Teller. He was in fact hounded out of the University of Alaska and black-balled in most other American universities. On January 22, 1962, his dean told him to kindly take his snow studies elsewhere—and not come back.

January sunrises arrive late, if at all, in the subarctic mountains. It was past eleven in the morning before the first glint of sunshine struck the surface of fresh-fallen snow. Around the column crystal were millions similar to itself—some stubbier, some longer—plus countless stellar crystals, hexagonal plates, needles and irregular ice pellets. All had undergone unique histories of creation and change during their fall from the sky. As the sunlight grew stronger, this still blanket of mixed snow began to take on a wealth of winter colors. Having traveled unperturbed for 150 million kilometers, the white rays from the sun now split into glittering pinpoints of sapphire, emerald, amethyst and ruby. Before two o'clock the snow surface became flat and featureless once again as the sun slid behind a knifelike ridge to the southwest. Stillness and shadow reigned over the alpine amphitheater.

Unaided by mechanical buffeting from the wind or thermal stress from the sun, the pristine crystals began to decompose. Mass self-destruction proceeded at various rates depending on the frailty of each crystal. The finest of stellar crystals were the first to go. In the exquisite architecture of their lacy arms lay the seeds of their own destruction. Their intricate frames and large surface-area-to-volume ratio were energetically unstable, a condition that the laws of thermodynamics would not tolerate for long. Within twenty-four hours their filigree margins became rounded and smooth as molecules of water vapor moved from the tips of the arms and refroze towards the crystals' more stable centers. As if too beautiful to last, the stellar crystals contracted and collapsed. Over the next two weeks their arms were reduced to even-edged blobs displaying all the elegance of bowling pins.

Meanwhile the column crystal, though structurally much sounder, also succumbed to nature's campaign against the orderly arrangement of molecules. The six well-defined edges of the column lost all their sharpness within a week of the crystal's landing. Within a month its hollow core had collapsed in response to further energetic downshifts and the pressure of fresh snow layers above. By late January the former column crystal and all that fell with it sixty nights earlier had been transformed into old snow lying within the dense middle layers of the snowpack. Regardless of original shape or life history, all crystals were reduced, more or less, to the most energetically ideal shape available to nature: an undifferentiated sphere.

Pruitt's time in Alaska, though aborted unexpectedly, helped him come to grips with an issue he felt was one of the main obstacles barring snow from a prominent place on the agenda of northern research. This was the issue of language. Common street terms for snow, such as *fluff*, *crud*, *sugar* and *corn*, were certainly of no use to Pruitt. Nor was the limited vocabulary of the weather office. "In my work in the North," Pruitt complains, "I have found that the official meteorological words for snow are woefully inadequate to describe its phases." Though the Russians had made enthusiastic headway in this area, their snow classifications tended to be needlessly complex and hopelessly unpronounceable.

Consequently Pruitt turned to the native peoples of the

A pagoda-shaped crystal of fragile pukak *constructed out of what looks like miniature glass logs.* (PHOTO: WILSON BENTLEY)

North, whose rich vocabulary of snow words reflects an intimate and practical knowledge of snow developed over thousands of years. One glossary of snow words used by tundra-dwelling Inuit contains over one hundred terms that describe subtle differences in snow that most southerners would not know if they tripped over them. Their words account for, among other things, the origin, texture, shape, density, age, utility and moisture content of snow. They have one word for snowdrifts formed by a northeast wind and another for those formed by a northwest wind. They have a word for the best kind of snow to chink cracks in drafty igloos. They have a word for "small pillar like protrusions of snow formed after the soft snow around animal tracks has been eroded by a blizzard." The language of snow is no less elaborate among taiga-dwelling native peoples, which were of special interest to Pruitt. Of all the languages he examined, the one that best matched his own observations and research needs was that of the so-called Forest Eskimo, who lived among the spruce in the Kobuk Valley of northwestern Alaska.

Annui: falling snow.

Api: snow on the ground not yet touched by the wind.

Qali: snow that sticks to the branches of trees.

Upsik: snow changed by the wind into a firm mass.

Qaminiq: a bowl-shaped hollow of thin snow around the base of a tree.

Pukak: the fragile layer of large loosely spaced crystals at the bottom of the snowpack.

Such snow words, first voiced by the Kobuk Valley native people, have become synonymous with the name and work of W.O. Pruitt.

Aboriginal leaders across the top of the continent have personally congratulated Pruitt for his liberal use of native languages to portray snow phenomena. On the other hand this practice has raised the academic hackles of many physicists and meteorologists. According to Pruitt, "They welcome the use of Latin or Greek names or symbols when writing about snow phenomena but have closed minds when we use aboriginal names." Pruitt once had a paper rejected from a so-called official publication on snow because he insisted on using native terminology for which there was no English or French equivalent. Though miffed he did not complain for long. The same paper was soon accepted as a chapter in a more mainstream book that received a much wider audience among more open-minded readers.

Winter locks into the boreal forest. (PHOTO: TESSA MACINTOSH)

As public servants most meteorologists are paid to look at snow with only two main questions in mind: How much will fall and when? Pruitt learned very early that such weather information is next to useless in predicting how boreal plants and animals will fare through the winter. He discovered for instance that during two winters with much the same weather, small mammal populations under the snow could exhibit vastly different mortalities, flourishing one year and floundering the next. He discovered that conditions within the snow-cover often have little to do with what we call weather. Turning his back on standard meteorological data, he discovered that what really mattered ecologically were things like the timing of snow's arrival and departure, the rate of its accumulation, its thickness, its density and its relative temperatures. Pruitt's fast-growing inventory of field data showed that these variables were closely linked to the biological welfare of snow-dwelling creatures.

Winter after winter Pruitt's meticulous snow studies confirmed that far from being a uniform, two-dimensional blanket on the ground, snow cover represented a multistory mosaic of microhabitats that had widely varying suitabilities for both animals and plants. It was the vehicle of native snow words that allowed him to convey this image systematically and precisely to sympathetic colleagues and students who had an ear for his unique perspective. Consider *qali*, he would tell them, those arboreal canopies of snow. What are they worth in the economy of nature? They insulate chickadees and owls, squirrels and snowshoe hares from the infinite heat sink of an open sky. They bend and sometimes break branches, bringing additional food within reach of many herbivores. They influence the shape and vigor of trees. Or think about *qaminiq*, those snow shadows beneath the trees. What happens there? Small mammals avoid them because their thin snow offers little insulating warmth or protection from predators. As winter fades, *qaminiq* become islands of spring, exposing seeds and insects to small birds in an otherwise snowy landscape. And what of the *pukak* layer, warm and loose and out of sight? What is its ecological significance? Living in a thermally stable environment, small mammals can tunnel easily through its delicate crystals. It yields also to the paws of moose, deer and caribou searching for plants beneath the snow. In mountainous regions it is called avalanche snow because, on steep slopes, *pukak*'s delicate architecture offers little resistance to gravity.

Pruitt has a soft spot for *pukak*. "I am more fascinated by *pukak* than by any other kind of snow-cover. You have to get down on your belly, necessarily with a magnifier and light reflector in order to appreciate pukak. It is so fragile, so beautiful and so important in the lives of small herbivores, small carnivores and invertebrates." Long ago he concluded that if it were not for the *pukak* layer, large parts of the northern forest would be devoid of voles, mice and shrews; they are physiologically incapable of surviving winter anywhere else. The ecological implications of this scenario are almost unthinkable because so many food chains are propped up somewhere along the line by small mammals. Such unsung natural connections fuel Pruitt's passion for snow and are at the heart of his special brand of boreal ecology.

Throughout the last half of February the dry arctic air mass and warm muggy Pacific air mass were locked in aerial combat as they struggled for supremacy over northwestern Canada. Their regular sallies back and forth over the mountains brought cold still weather one day followed by blizzards the next. An even surface of fresh fluffy snow would drape the mountain only briefly this time of year. Soon after falling it was blasted into a wind crust, carved into dunes or sublimated into vapor by cold, thirsty air from the north. Or it was buried under half a meter of heavy wet snow blown in from the south. The story of these weather fluctuations was recorded in the changing densities and textures of the snowpack's layers as truly as the rise and fall of oceans are recorded in the mountain's sedimentary rocks.

Far removed from the wide flux of weather occurring at

the surface was a round grain of ice that housed a micro-scopic fleck of volcanic ash from the Philippines. It had set-tled near the bottom of the snowpack, where heat flowing up from the earth warmed the air spaces around the grain to a steady minus five—twenty degrees warmer than the prevail-ing temperature at the surface. The ice grain shrank in the heat as it gave up its water molecules to the warm, rising vapor. Finally it disappeared, releasing the ash particle to the surrounding snow.

Molecules of water vapor moved through the snow along a thermal gradient of ever-cooler temperatures. They vapor-ized, then froze again, passing upwards from grain to grain in a hand-to-hand sort of fashion. New crystals were under construction, some of them growing quite large. These were *pukak* crystals that bore utterly no resemblance to any kind of freshly fallen crystals or coarse old grains. Instead they looked like hollow pyramids or pagodas built from minute logs of glass. In this way bottom layers of old snow completely van-ished and were reconstructed as *pukak* crystals, one of which had wrapped itself around the errant fleck of ash.

By mid-March there was real warmth in the noon sun as it bathed the mountain's jagged brow and most of the snowy amphitheater below. The amplitude of daily swings in tem-perature increased dramatically. Nights of minus thirty degrees were followed by days of minus five. Near the base of the snowpack, thermal stability still reigned, though physical stability was fast deteriorating. The loose bonds between *pukak* crystals neared the breaking point as the heavier, denser layers above crept imperceptibly downslope under the inces-sant strain of gravity. This movement, now measurable in microns per hour, was building up forces that, if let loose, could exceed magnitudes of several tons per square meter.

Subtle shifts in surface tension caused spontaneous ruptures in the delicately poised *pukak* layer. Multiple fissures formed deep within the snowpack. Small random surface slides moving no more than a few wheelbarrow's worth of snow at a time gave expression to the dwindling mechanical strength below. Amidst these stresses and strains, the *pukak* crystal now housing the ash fleck remained intact. It was in fact still growing new latticework though not as quickly as it had during the consistent cold of midwinter.

On the night of the March full moon, a translucent veil of scalelike altostratus clouds moved in over the mountains. By morning the sky had turned a granite gray. The clouds thickened throughout the day and much of the next night until they finally opened just before dawn. At first they dropped cold dry snow in the form of fine needles and tiny bullet-shaped columns. Several hours into the storm, strong moist winds suddenly encroached from the southwest, changing the snowfall into pulpy wet pellets. In all, this one storm dumped thirty-five centimeters of new snow on the mountain in less than twenty-four hours. High winds and temperatures just below freezing continued long after the snow stopped, cementing the heavy upper layers into a thick cohesive slab. Though internally stabilized by the wind, the upper layers were now poised for mass motion on top of a hair-trigger platform of loose dry snow. Not far below was a stressed-out foundation of *pukak*.

The detonator was a half-ton chunk of limestone that popped off the mountaintop. One sunny afternoon in late March, a trickle of meltwater dribbled into a critical seam joining boulder to bluff. That night it froze, muscling deeper into the crack as it expanded. The next morning, minutes after the sun struck the broken rock, the mountain let it drop. A union of seventy million years ended as the boulder gave in to gravity and made a brief rolling free fall through space.

Still rolling, it careened down a snow-free talus slope of frost-shattered rock, bounced violently off another boulder, then disappeared with a soft thud into the mountain's snowy shoulder. It landed a few centimeters from the ash-cored *pukak* crystal, which by now resembled a stretched and twisted staircase due to the mounting stresses from above. It was among the first of several billion crystals to shatter when the rock hit. In rapid succession dull booms rippled out from the impact crater as the *pukak* layer collapsed and let go of its weak hold on the underlying bedrock. All pent-up tensions in the huge snow slab above found release as it disengaged explosively from the mountain. Where it came unhinged the snow slab was two hundred meters across. It dropped *en masse* from the forty-degree slope, accelerating rapidly on a fresh dry bed of needles and bullets, which offered all the resistance of ball bearings. At full speed the avalanche rumbled down the mountain with the power of fifty diesel locomotives. It lost no momentum as it entered a fan-shaped chute just below the tree line.

Caught up in the wake of the avalanche, the smashed skeleton of the *pukak* crystal was carried half a kilometer down the mountain. It finally came to rest on the flat valley floor buried inside a five-meter-high mound of disintegrated snow. Twenty seconds passed before the echo of the avalanche's roar stopped bouncing off the surrounding mountain flanks. Within two hours the huge mound of snow at the base of the avalanche chute had fully recrystallized and turned as hard as rock.

No serious students of snow will master their craft by reading Pruitt's many scientific papers on the subject—or anyone else's for that matter. They must make their discoveries firsthand by direct knee-deep participation in the white stuff itself. They must experience as many of its infinite faces as possible by contemplating its surface and probing its depths. They must learn to read the signs of perpetual change in the snowpack and know how to recognize the living and nonliving agents that cause them. They must abandon all their prejudices and preconceptions about snow and look at it afresh. "I believe recording details of snow-cover should be a part of all field biological research in Canada," says Pruitt. What better place to do it than a biological research station of one's own design?

The University of Manitoba's Taiga Biological Station exists largely because of Pruitt's passion for snow. It is set unobtrusively within a wilderness park of boreal bush and bedrock 240 kilometers northeast of Winnipeg. Atikaki Provincial Park is officially described as "one of the most magnificent examples of shield country anywhere," complete with several rushing rivers that "dish out thrills on par with the Snake and Colorado." Pruitt has a special fondness for this country, and in 1973 he came here to select the site for his station. He built the simple log cabins with significant help from compliant students (read "slave labor" or "volunteers," depending on your point of view). True to his affinity for things Scandinavian, he added a sauna soon after the bare necessities of camp were in place. Because of tight money and great distances to affordable supply centers, the entire camp was a case of building something from nothing. Rampant scrounging of materials, from windows to outhouse toilet seats, turned everyone involved into pack rats—an acquired skill that some of Pruitt's students continue to take pride in.

When part of the camp was destroyed by a forest fire in the late seventies, Pruitt recruited more students to help him cut, peel and haul logs out of the bush, then ferry them seventeen kilometers across Wallace Lake. His own cabin is no

All but Pruitt's beard is enveloped in a steamy winter campfire.
(Photo: Rick Riewe)

less austere than the bunkhouses occupied by his students. It is here that Pruitt and his wife, Erna, occasionally put their moccasined feet up in front of the wood stove to savor a hot nip of Captain Morgan's spiced rum. He often cooks and shares meals with his students and itinerant guests, not all of whom are invited. A few years ago Pruitt's favorite frying pan suffered a broad dent, still visible, when his wife brought it soundly down upon the head of a black bear that had stolen into the cook tent around breakfast time. In course calendars Pruitt describes the research station as "a purposely primitive field facility." Students are invited to join him in studying "adaptations of mammals to boreal environments, particularly winter and snow conditions."

All of Pruitt's students are expected to spend a good part of at least one winter in the bush. Dr. Rick Riewe was Pruitt's first graduate student and has followed closely in his mentor's snowshoe tracks for about thirty winters. Now a professor of zoology himself, Riewe says, "Bill believes that it is necessary for his students to live in primitive accommodations so that they are in tune with the environment rather than live in a modern field station which insulates them from the environment. I agree with this completely. Quite often the most useful skills we acquire from Bill are bush skills." Among the many skills Riewe gained at Pruitt's side were how to concoct home brew in the bush and sew a tobacco pouch out of a moose scrotum. "He taught us to be innovative and self-sufficient. He constantly challenged us."

Another former student of Pruitt's puts it more bluntly. "He put the fear of God into us," admits Rosanna Strong, who years later chose to live with her husband in an isolated subarctic cabin North of Sixty. "He was very active and had very high expectations. But he never demanded more from us than he could do himself." While visiting colleagues slept soundly in their bunks, Pruitt and selected "volunteers" would get up at all hours of the night and tromp down well-packed snowshoe trails in search of voles and shrews. In the name of good science and humane trapping, all small-mammal traps had to be checked every two hours regardless of the night's temperatures or the students' temperaments. On a good night they could handle sixty to seventy traps per hour with little time left for sleep.

On such nights those still snug and smug in their sleeping bags invariably would be woken well before dawn by Pruitt's clarion call to breakfast. "Wakey, wakey, wakey. It's minus forty at the bottom of the hill. A beautiful day! A beautiful day! Where're the cooks? Where're the cooks?" Many students observed that the cheeriness in his delivery varied inversely with temperature—the colder the morning, the cheerier his voice—though no scientific paper was ever published verifying this phenomenon.

Snow student reading wildlife clues on the forest's snowy sketch pad. (Photo: Tessa Macintosh)

Feared more than midwinter "trap nights" was the notorious Pruitt biathlon in which the Snowman tested the outer limits of his student's mental and physical stamina. He insisted that at least once in their field apprenticeship, all his students don cross-country skis and head off down the trail to scavenge for ecological clues. In the early days Pruitt supplied all the skis himself. They were wooden with gangly cable bindings and renowned for their impressive dimensions. "Pruitt planks" they called them. "They were easily twenty feet long and two feet wide!" recalls one former student. Thus equipped, his pupils spent the better part of a day dashing through the snow, trying to follow their professor's crafty instructions, measuring this, recording that. Whose teeth cleanly severed this willow branch? Whose paws made those paired evenly spaced prints along the riverbank? What is the temperature range within this snowdrift? What kind of spruce is this and what adaptations does it have to survive at minus forty? Who made that snow tunnel? Who dropped that scat? With frost-nipped fingers and numbed minds students adapted as best they could to the cold and the rigors of bore-al ecology taught by a master. "I survived a Pruitt biathlon," was the proud maxim of all his graduates. "He opened my eyes to so much," remembers Strong. "I never would have come to know and love the boreal forest as I do now."

A series of late-winter blizzards dumped thirty centime-ters of snow on the mountain valley. The additional weight further compacted the mound of cementlike snow at the bottom of the avalanche chute. The snow mass became denser and more coherent as air spaces among the old round-ed snow grains shrank and new molecular bonds formed among them. Deep inside the snow mass, the ash fleck was housed in a smoothly furrowed lump of clear ice the shape of a sheep's head. This irregular grain of ice was a far-distant cousin to the six-sided column that originally transported the ash back to earth and the delicate *pukak* crystal that carried it down the mountain. No longer a separate component of the snow, the lump had bonded with several neighboring grains. Together they had the shape of a cluster of grapes long past their prime.

Then, for the first time in seven months, the temperature at the snow surface rose above zero. On clear days the sheltered valley floor, which had remained in shadow for half of that time, now received over eight hours of direct sunlight. Although 80 percent of this light was reflected back into outer space, infrared radiation penetrated several centimeters into the snow, shifting the net radiation balance into the positive. The snow mass began to melt. By day, meltwater began percolating down through the snow, then refreezing at night. The snow mass soon became saturated with water, becoming heavier by the day. The pores among the snow grains shrank farther still, becoming almost microscopic. Continued over many months, this process would transform this footprint of an avalanche into a small but credible glacier.

But soon melting got the upper hand over freezing, and the glacier was not to be. Under starry skies the temperature continued to dip below zero most nights, creating a crust of firm ice on the surface. During the first few hours of the morning, this clear window over the snow acted just like greenhouse glass. The trapped heat below penetrated deeply into the snow, forming warm hollows bridged by an ice layer above.

By early afternoon the ice crust vanished. Warm southwest breezes swept down the valley, causing widespread sublimation at the snow surface. As the downward flow of heat finally reached the underlying feather moss, up came the snow fleas to engage in their erratic spring mating dance. Thousands of their black wiggling bodies peppered the surface, hastening the absorption of heat and the melting of snow. So did the dust particles, pollen spores and other nuclei around which each original snow crystal had formed. So did twigs, needles and other wind-blown debris that landed on the surface. All these slowly sank as they absorbed heat, then radiated it to the adjacent snow.

Spring melt carves its way through a mountain stream. (PHOTO: CHRIS O'BRIEN)

It was a lone pellet from a snowshoe hare that ultimately broke the temporary alliance between ash and ice. The grain of ice was now barely distinguishable from its neighbors, having all but merged with them during repeated floods of meltwater. Directly above it, heat radiating from the dark hare pellet bore a vertical tube down through the snow. Just before the shadow of a mountain stole across the surface, the snow tube reached the level of the ice grain. There was sufficient heat given off by the hare pellet to mobilize the grain's constituent water molecules to a higher energetic state. Millions of molecular bonds broke within seconds as the solid ice grain vaporized into thin air. Ten days later the ash particle it once housed was flushed from the decaying mound of snow at the base of the avalanche chute. It came to rest briefly on a fire-charred spruce log that teetered over the bank of a small stream channel. Meltwater from south-facing slopes above soon flooded the winding channel, swamping the spruce log and carrying the ash particle into the headwaters of the South Nahanni River. Six weeks later it was halfway down the Mackenzie. On the last day of August it settled to the bottom of the Beaufort Sea.

Extreme situations can bring prevailing attitudes about a controversial subject into clear focus. The subject of snow is no exception. Few northern Europeans who lived through it will ever forget the winter of '62. From Scotland to Siberia, severe blizzards, deep snow and record low temperatures severely crippled all forms of transportation for months. Schools were closed for weeks on end. Many senior citizens expired in their beds, succumbing once and for all to the cold. Millions of people greeted Europe's snowiest winter in one hundred years with clenched teeth and raised fists. Meanwhile, unknown to all but a small circle of German zoologists, the region's vole populations, snugged in under all that snow, were enjoying unprecedented abundance and weight gains. They were breeding like rabbits and fattening like pigs.

After watching all kinds of winters dump snow on all kinds of people across the circumpolar world, Pruitt concludes that "the reactions of various human cultures to snow vary from a welcoming acceptance to near hysteria when it falls. The very abundance of snow seems to have suppressed almost all but the negative aspects of getting rid of it as quickly as possible. In the literature of the sciences that ought to be most concerned, there is even yet little to suggest that snow is a major element in the environment of life."

Yet as the Atomic Energy Commission (AEC) learned years ago, Pruitt is adept at swimming against the current of mainstream opinions. His work as both scientist and crusader proclaims—rigorously and unabashedly—the many virtues of snow and emphasizes its pivotal role in boreal ecology. "Indeed," says Pruitt, "one might accurately say that boreal ecology *is* the study of snow." This conclusion, the upshot of his research, did not come easily or quickly to him. According to one handbook for mountaineers, who, like other snow-adapted mammals, must know how to read snow to stay alive, "the repertoire of snow is too large for all its tricks to be encountered in one year—or in ten. Complete familiarity with the behavior of snow, if attainable, would require a lifetime." After devoting half a century of winters to the study of snow, Pruitt probably knows as much about the subject as any one man could.

On a snowy evening in November 1989, during a gala ceremony at the Lester B. Pearson Building in downtown Ottawa, Dr. William Obadiah Pruitt Jr., professor of zoology, was presented with a medal. It was part of the Northern Science Award earned by those who had achieved scholarly acclaim in northern scientific research. In pinning the medal on the professor's light brown corduroy jacket, the Honourable Pierre H. Cadieux, Minister of Indian Affairs and Northern Development, announced that Dr. Pruitt had "instilled in many of his students a love and respect for the land and animals of the North." He went on to herald him as the "father of North American Boreal Ecology." Along with the medal, Cadieux slipped Pruitt a check for five thousand dollars. Pruitt seized this moment as an opportunity to yet again come to the aid of his students and his research, both of which lately had been strapped for cash.

In no uncertain terms he told his benefactors how in Canada, snow research has not been granted the same priority it has in other northern countries. He told them how grants for northern field studies were increasingly hard to come by and how guaranteed multiyear research support was now a thing of the past. He told them that "the starvation of northern biological research" was having a severe impact on essential long-term research at his beloved Taiga Biological Station. Field studies, including those on snow ecology, were persevering on a nickel and dime basis by the grace of a dwindling private trust and meager grants in the order of one to three thousand dollars. Just in case his funders weren't getting the message, Pruitt, in a wry show of thanks, promised to put his money where his mouth was. "The whole situation is unhealthy for northern science. That is why the five-thousand-dollar prize accompanying this award is so valuable and appreciated—it means I can support a student in the field for almost a year."

Pruitt suspects that things might have turned out differently if not for the superabundance of Canadian snow. "Generations of graduate students would doubtless have received degrees for research into the properties and potential uses of snow, if snowflakes were rare objects that were obtainable only by expensive and involved laboratory processes."

In spite of the paltry blessings offered to Pruitt from scientific granting agencies, he remains cautiously optimistic about the future of snow research. "I think my scientific publications may have had some effect in opening colleagues' eyes to the role snow-cover plays in natural processes." He suggests that his greatest contribution to science is the invention of a snow index that links particular snow conditions to the habits and habitat preferences of various animals. Pruitt sees tremendous potential in this slick and simple tool. "I feel that if we could devise a snow index for each species of mammal in Canada, we would have a powerful tool for managing the species." His wish is that the snow index will become as common and accepted within the scientific community as pH is as an indicator of acidity.

Meanwhile, by contributing to the popular press, Pruitt continues to open the eyes of Canadian masses to his gospel on snow. In his now classic *Wild Harmony: The Cycle of Life in the Northern Forest*, Pruitt pioneered a unique kind of prose that places the reader behind the eyes, ears and nose of that archetypal snow dweller, the tundra vole.

> The new snow covered the layer of birch seeds and hid them from the small birds. The added weight of the fresh snow compacted the middle layers of the *api*. As the crystals squeezed together and broke, the cover creaked and groaned. A foraging vole would stop and huddle, ears twitching, and then resume its errand. The sounds breached the even tenor of life under the snow. An additional disturbance was the faint scent of birch carbohydrate that occasionally filtered down from above. Some voles dug upward through the layers of snow. One layer was easily tunneled, the next was harder; no two were alike. When a vole reached the seed-rich layer it drove a horizontal drift along it and devoured every seed. Without the traditional scent boundaries to restrain them, some voles encountered

their fellows directly. What squeaking and scuffling as the asocial animals repulsed invaders!

Knowing that some of the best science springs from the heart Pruitt hopes that by tunneling his readers into the snow and helping them appreciate the living world within it, he will inspire some to follow his trail into applied field research. "I firmly believe," he writes in the prologue to *Wild Harmony*, "that such appreciation is a necessary prerequisite to the more intensive ecological research which must follow."

Still, there are some that have yet to wake up to the strong light Pruitt throws onto snow. For instance one of his colleagues resolutely insists that there can be no invertebrate activity under the snow. The idea that any living thing—from ice worms and snow fleas to tundra voles and pygmy shrews—could actually be *down there*, alive and well, remains inconceivable to those who view snow not as a benevolent life-supporting blanket but as a sterile and suffocating shroud.

Subarctic winters often die in prolonged fits and starts. The thaw begins in earnest, then a cold spell sets in, then more thawing followed by another cold spell. This equivocating of seasons brings to Pruitt's mind an image of winter retreating "to just beyond the hill," still able to suck warmth from the land "in a last defiant gesture." Frequent dips above and below zero play havoc with snow structure, pitting and icing the surface, collapsing basement layers and saturating all from top to bottom with cold dripping water. Voles don't like this. Wholesale freezing and thawing of soggy snow, if it continues for many days, can lock voles out of their food stores. When temperatures dive yet again, vole mortality rises as they become entombed in rotten, ice-sheathed snow or succumb to exposure on open snowless ground. Caribou, a creature of winter if there ever was one, also can suffer during the season's drawn-out demise. Recently on Bathurst Island, Northwest Territories, over 450 caribou starved because they could not dig through a rain-soaked layer of deep snow. Several died in their tracks. Weeks later, biologists found some of them still standing with their legs encased in bloody ice-layered snow.

Koyukon elders from subarctic Alaska speak grimly of the hardships brought not so long ago by long-shouldered springs. Snowshoe hares were next to impossible to catch because the ice-covered snow let them bound willy-nilly off their established trails, where the empty snares hung. During such springs moose and caribou could hear hunters coming kilometers away as they approached on the noisy crust. "Every day they would just pray," said one woman who lived through the frightful spring of 1937. "It was so hard for them to catch animals." She remembered how her people spent day after day on their hands and knees scratching the snowless ground around the base of large spruce trees. They were looking for migratory songbirds that had dropped dead from the cold. Her people survived that spring cold spell on a diet consisting mostly of warblers and sparrows.

It's no wonder that like many northern mammals and snow-adapted natives, Pruitt gets a little edgy during the spring melt. "He doesn't like the heat," says one of his graduates. "Besides it wrecks all those marvelous snow crystals he likes to study." After just a few of his classes Pruitt's freshman students quickly come to understand, perhaps even endorse, the revolutionary sentiments behind the bumper sticker on his office door: *STAMP OUT SUMMER!*

LIVING DOWN UNDER

It is safest in winter when it is in snug dens protected
by thick layers of ice, out of sight and out of reach.
—*Earl Hilfiker,* Beavers: Water, Wildlife and History

When I was about eight years old, my father brought home a huge clunking reel-to-reel tape recorder which launched me into a lifelong fascination with sound pictures. My brother and I used to go to great lengths to capture just the right squeak on a door or clatter of dishes when creating the palette of sounds needed for our basement-produced radio plays.

Over twenty-five years later, my first real gig with radio began in the outdoors, a setting wonderfully rich with sound. Often nature freely supplied just the right sounds on cue while we broadcast live. Like the time two tundra swans magically came honking overhead just as I had finished saying, "and if we're lucky we might see some tundra swans." During a show on wind, the breezes got so strong I had to remove one of my socks and put it over the microphone so we could make ourselves heard over the rumbling. And whether we wanted them or not, ravens seemed to get a word or two in edgewise during most shows. To these gratuitous sounds we often added our own to help draw listeners farther outside: a crackling fire, a goose call, drilling an ice auger through meter-thick ice, digging into permafrost, the sound of berries kerplunking into a tin can.

In darkness and in light, in rain and snow, we broadcast live and outside for over one hundred Monday mornings. Debuting in a marsh on a sunny May morning in 1992, our nature series was only supposed to last six to eight weeks. "But," as CBC anchor man Randy Henderson put it on our last show, "it got so popular, Jamie kept coming back." Teachers, hungry for northern science material, often asked me for taped copies of their favorite shows. Sadly I had to report that no such tapes existed. Such is the fleeting nature of radio. Regular listeners from all walks of life would sometimes approach me with such statements as, "I'd never really looked at snow before hearing your show," or "I was time-traveling with you when you were talking about those ancient volcanoes," or "Were you guys *really* bungee-jumping into that gravel pit?" Even several preschoolers, I understand, were regular fans of the series. One called me Mr. Mosquito (rhymes with Bastedo) for a long while after one of our more probing bug shows.

Inspired by such public interest, the radio series ranged widely across nature's infinite colors. I took listeners to some of my favorite outdoor haunts—a wetland "polluted with ducks," a high windswept cliff edge or a hushed sanctuary of mature spruce. I had them look afresh at some familiar aspect of northern nature—the raven, the jackfish and, of course, snow. I shared with them new insights into things I'd never thought much about before: how subarctic plants avoid freezing solid, how diamonds are formed, how much a glacier can weigh or how beavers survive winter locked under the ice. I came to see my role as a kind of torchbearer into nature, helping people find the light switches to a hitherto darkened art gallery.

6:00 A.M. Showday. My brain was half awake as I lay idly in bed waiting for the alarm to go off. It's dark in the frigid

December dawn in Yellowknife. When we go on air for this week's show we'll still barely be able to see our notes under the dim purplish orange light of what some call morning. Last week, equipped with Christmas bells and high-powered binoculars, we had been stalking the elusive reindeer from the roof of an eighteen-story condominium in downtown Yellowknife. Between the low light conditions and howling wind tearing our notes from our mitts, it's a wonder that we ever pulled that show off. But I learned long ago that the show must go on no matter what.

The shrill electronic beeping of the alarm blasted me off the mattress and across the bedroom floor. I groped for the kill switch on the first of three alarm clocks that I had set ten minutes apart. I had upgraded from one clock to three after the time our technician, Alan Beck, had to phone to wake me eight minutes before air time.

I dressed quietly and quickly in the darkness, slipping on one pair of long underwear, then another. I always dress for minus forty for midwinter shows. Chattering teeth make for poor public radio.

Today's show: how beavers face the challenges of winter. While my snowmobile warmed up I loaded my four-meter-long canvas-sided toboggan with all the equipment needed to tell this story: one large bucket, ten liters of bottled water, one Spartan apple, one sterling silver table knife, my wife's favorite garden trowel and, oh yes, a head lamp.

I dashed into the house for a quick pit stop of cranberry-bran muffins and a strong steaming cup of Earl Grey tea. I grabbed an old towel on the way out the door, then saddled up. My noisy exit from the neighborhood created a large wake of barking sled dogs behind me. I stopped five minutes later in front of a burned-out trailer—Number 33—near the edge of town. Alan Beck was already there—quiet, reliable, unshakable Alan, who brings a technical security blanket to each show. We had done enough shows together for me to know that behind those dark curly locks and boyish grin was a ruthless guardian of the airwaves, always ready to trounce upon any technical gremlins that might come our way and thus shield the listening public from such evils as white static, rolling hums or, worst of all, dead air. I helped Alan dump his gear into the toboggan: a blue canvas backpack, what seemed like a few kilometers of black cable, three radio headsets and a microphone that he said probably cost more than my snowmobile. "Go easy on the bumps," he told me.

Beside the trailer was a narrow path that cut though a jungle of willows and juvenile spruce. It led to a small lake fringed with tall golden cattails. I drove across the lake to a large snow-covered mound about eight meters across and two meters high. Inside that mound, alive and well, was a family of beavers. Of the many nearby habitats occupied by beavers, we chose this site for three reasons: the ambient noise environment was relatively clean, it had a nice wilderness feel to it (I need that for inspiration) and it was less than a seven-minute drive from the CBC North studio.

The instant the 8:30 A.M. news began, Randy Henderson, host of CBC's *Mackenzie Morning* show, leaped from his studio anchor desk into his lumbering Aerostar van and drove directly toward trailer Number 33. A twenty-year veteran of northern radio, Randy welcomed the excitement of these remote outdoor broadcasts. "They give me incentive to stay awake till the end of my shift," he once told me off air. His alarm clock goes off three hours before mine.

Leaving Alan alone on the lake, I returned to the abandoned trailer to pick up Randy. I left my noisy machine running while I paced back and forth on the road to keep warm. Across the street in another trailer, someone parted the window curtains briefly, then immediately let the dog out, a large German Shepherd, presumably to scare me away. It trotted straight for me with its ears, tail and dorsal fur erect. I froze. I could not remember whether I should or should not look this aggressor in the eye. At that moment, Randy's headlights intercepted the dog's train of thought (and mine), and it took off into the bush behind me. With eight minutes left before air time, we did little more than exchange hellos as Randy settled quickly into the toboggan. His unperturbed smile and eastern style goatee gave him a Buddha-like demeanor amidst the smoke and noise and haste of my mission. He pulled his parka ruff up over his Montreal Expos ball cap, then gave me two thumbs up.

We arrived at the beaver lodge with just two minutes to spare. Alan was absorbed in a final sound check and completely ignored us. With hands bared, he was busily flicking switches and twiddling knobs on the marvelous invention that let us broadcast live to the entire western Arctic: a powerful remote transmitter that fit neatly into his trim blue pack. When closed, this device would not appear out of place on a weekend camping trip except for the long silver antenna poking out the top.

Clockwork. I quickly ushered Randy over to a patch of snow I had stomped down beside the lodge. At our feet were my carefully laid out props. Alan handed him the microphone, a headset and a digital chronometer carefully synchronized to the studio's master clock. The southeastern sky blushed orange while the night's last dance of northern lights faded in the west. A rising breeze from the north brought the wind chill equivalent to about minus thirty-five. Two ravens alighted on a lakeside spruce tree. They looked down at us expectantly as if settling in to watch the show.

With thirty seconds to go, I flicked on my head lamp and

There are beavers down there, believe it or not. Dried cattails in foreground. (PHOTO: TESSA MACINTOSH)

dusted the snow off my notes. I took a few deep breaths, cleared my throat, then clammed up. Randy gave me a friendly wiggle of his eyebrows, then started talking into his microphone.

"Welcome back folks. This is *Mackenzie Morning* broadcasting to you live from the bush with naturalist Jamie Bastedo. Good morning, Jamie."

"A frosty good morning to you, Randy."

About two minutes into the interview I made two disturbing observations. First, the screen on the chronometer attached to Randy's clipboard read 00:00:00. Time had stopped dead thanks to frozen batteries. How would we know when it was 08:58:30, time to sign off and give Peter Gzowski a chance to preview his *Morningside* show before the nine o'clock news? And second, the left side of Randy's nose was turning a deathly white. I gestured to it, but because his hands were occupied with clipboard and mike, all he could do was smile and shrug. In spite of our dead chronometer and Randy's frost-nipped nose, the show did go on as we knew it must.

The beaver's world around us appeared dormant and still. The lodge, the lake, the dam, the rocky shore were all blended together under a uniform shroud of midwinter snow. The scene made Randy skeptical that the three of us were not entirely alone.

"It's probably been over four months since I last saw a beaver swimming around," said Randy. "You've assured me that they don't herd together and migrate south for the winter." He let go one of his well-polished chuckles. "I find it hard to believe that beavers don't hibernate, that they're active all winter and might well be swimming around below our feet as we speak. What exactly *is* going on down there, Jamie?"

"This is indeed a picture of snowy stillness," I said. "Almost deathlike from our point of view, as if this whole lake ecosystem were locked into suspended animation for the winter. But there is a bustle of life in this lodge and below the meter of ice that we're standing on. In a sense we are worlds apart from the beaver, yet we are physically very close."

"They're probably listening to us right now."

"No doubt. During the coldest part of the winter, northern beavers do indeed sleep a lot—don't *you*?"

"I try my best."

"They lose their appetite. Their metabolism slows down and they stop growing. But as snug and secure as their winter world may seem, beavers can't just sleep it off. Hibernation is strictly out of the question. It would be suicidal. After several days of inactivity, their metabolic furnaces would shut down, resulting in a frozen huddle of beavers in a frozen lodge. Beavers must feed throughout the winter since they're not physiologically equipped for hibernation."

"They must have a big stash of food down there under the ice to last them through seven or eight months of winter."

"Very large. The first heavy frost of fall triggers something in the beaver's brain that makes it build a food pile. No fancy architecture here, not like their dams or lodges. It's basically just a big pile of sticks. They drag branches of aspen, birch and willow to deep water near the lodge entrance. As the pile grows, everything eventually sinks to the bottom, where they can get at it in the winter. They often cap the whole mass with alder branches—like alfalfa sprouts on top of a salad. Somebody once measured the weight of a monster food pile. It came to 380 kilograms—almost the weight of a small car."

"That's quite a salad."

"It's strictly a northern recipe. The California cousins of subarctic beavers have no idea how to build a food pile. Why should they? With no ice in the way they can dine on trees along the shore all year round. But the farther north you go, the thicker the ice, the longer the winters. . . ."

"The bigger the food pile."

"Exactly. But even so, by late winter the underwater larder of northern beavers can be bare. When this happens they either supplement their diet with aquatic plants or starve down there under the ice."

"Isn't it dark down there? How do they find their food?"

"They essentially live in a darkened world for months. With lots of snow on the ice and short winter days, the brightest day might give them only a dim, bluish light. They are locked away from the normal cues of light and dark, so they live mostly by the rhythm of their stomachs. They'll go out for a feed any time of day or night. Those beady little eyes are weak at the best of times, so they must have a pretty good navigation system on board. Like Zen monks they live in a small, orderly community apart from our world, sleeping when tired, eating when hungry."

"Do they actually munch on this stuff underwater?

"They often do and that in itself is quite an art. Have you ever tried eating something underwater, say, in the bathtub?

"Not recently."

"I wanted to demonstrate how difficult that is."

"Okay, Jamie. If you insist."

I kneeled down respectfully before the empty bucket. "You know how I like to enter into a creature's world. What I have here is a very large bucket. First I'm going to fill it with water—watch your microphone." I slopped the water into the pail as noisily as I could; this was, after all, live radio. Randy leaned cautiously over the bucket. I picked up the fast-freezing apple and table knife. "Of course anyone who has bobbed for apples at Halloween knows they float. Therefore, to replicate the challenge faced by a hungry beaver underwater, I'm going to stick this heavy table knife through the apple so it will sink." I plopped the whole affair into the water. "There. I'm ready."

"The things you do in the name of science, Jamie. I don't believe you're going to do this, but go ahead."

"It's not so cold today. And we're tucked out of the wind behind this beaver lodge. If it were forty below I'd probably just talk about it." I hung the towel on a stick protruding from the lodge. I took off my head lamp, hat and mitts. "Okay, I'm going to stick my head into this bucket and try, like a beaver, not only to bite off a piece of apple but to chew it and swallow it—all underwater. Are you ready, Randy?"

"As ready as I'll ever be, I guess."

"It's a rosy red Spartan down there. . . ."

"My favorite kind."

"Are you *sure* you're ready, Randy?"

"Go for it!" he said, vigorously pointing to the dead chronometer on his clipboard. Silent Alan, who normally stands well away from the action, stepped forward and held up five fingers in front of my still-dry face. I nodded, then cried, "Here goes!"

I can't remember if I had my eyes open. It didn't seem to matter. I felt strangely safe underwater though not the least bit hungry. After a few wholehearted lunges at the apple and some serious gurgling, I came up for air.

"It's very difficult to get a bite let alone eat the thing," I reported in a somewhat waterlogged voice. Then, back in . . . and out. "There! I managed to loosen a chunk. Now I'm going to try and eat it while still underwater." More gurgling and some unintelligible shouts. Randy released a few unrehearsed belly laughs. My experiment failed. I spluttered to the surface. "That's a tough act. I just could *not* swallow any apple down there."

"Quick, here's your towel," said Randy, throwing it over my head.

"Thanks for lifeguarding. What I am trying to illustrate here is how difficult it is for a land mammal like me to eat underwater."

"So what do beavers have that you don't?"

"It's one thing to chew off bark underwater; it's quite another to swallow it. Beavers can perform this trick thanks to a large, well-furred set of extra lips *behind* their front incisors. While those famous chisel-like teeth are peeling off the bark, the rear set of lips is tightly closed. No water gets in. The beaver doesn't drown—like I might have in that bucket. When it's time to swallow, the front lips close, then the back ones open and down goes the food. The whole process works like a set of boat locks along a canal, opening and closing in proper sequence."

"Besides this fancy mouth gear what other adaptations does the beaver have to help it survive under the ice?"

I gestured to the lodge. "Imagine an adult beaver snugged inside this very lodge. Its stomach grumbles. The two kits just devoured the lodge's last stores of freshly shredded bark as a midnight snack. Time to dine out. The instant the beaver's nose touches the water of the plunge hole, special flaps in its nostrils and ears automatically swing tightly shut, like the blowhole of a sounding whale. A clear protective membrane sweeps across its eyes."

"That's one watertight animal."

"Indeed. So there it goes, down through the tunnel and out into the murk. It swims a few meters, just below the ice, over to its food pile. It clamps its sharp little forepaws around an aspen log and starts chewing. This animal is in no particular hurry. It's not exerting itself much and has a comfortable fifteen-minute window before it needs a fresh supply of air."

"How does it manage that?"

"When you're underwater every heartbeat counts. As soon as the beaver goes into a dive, its heart rate automatically slows down by almost 80 percent. The only other mammals that can do this are whales. And for its size, the beaver has huge lungs. This adds up to incredibly efficient oxygen absorption. You and I exchange about 15 percent of the air in our lungs, the rest goes in and out with the oxygen untapped. A beaver on the other hand taps 75 percent of the air it inhales."

"Scuba tanks could become obsolete if we learned that trick."

"There's more. For dessert our beaver could choose to wander away from its food pile in search of some tasty aquatic plants. It could easily cover almost a kilometer of under-ice terrain before returning to the lodge. On the way out it might pause to carefully expel a large bubble of air below the ice. It can prolong its feeding time by inhaling its own bubbles on the way home."

"What good is stale air to a beaver?"

"It turns out that carbon dioxide dissolves in water almost thirty times faster than oxygen. This freshens up the bubbles by the time the beaver returns for a nip of air."

About this time in the broadcast, I noticed that Randy had dropped his clipboard in the snow and was repeatedly switching his microphone from one hand to the other, briefly shaking the one that was free. Numb fingers. I was glad to see that some color had returned to his nose. As for me, any hair dangling from under my hat was frozen solid. Alan stood aside in stoic silence.

"Is cold water a problem for beavers?"

"It definitely is. In spite of their wonderful well-oiled coats, beavers are surprisingly prone to what's called immersion hypothermia. While in that near-freezing water below our feet, heat is being sucked from their bodies up to three hundred times faster than in this lodge. Heaps of studies have been done on the beaver to try and figure out how they keep warm. Some animals like ravens and caribou can turn up the rate of their basal metabolism to compensate for energy lost to the cold. Not the beaver. Some animals like sea otters and ducks have a relatively waterproof body covering that insulates well even when wet. Not the beaver."

"So, how do they survive?"

"One unusual adaptation is what I call the pre-plunge warm-up. By implanting thermal transmitters into the bellies of free-living beavers, zoologists have discovered that their body temperature rises around half a degree three hours before the first dip of the day . . . or night, as the case may be. Somehow beavers know not to dive until after this warm-up period."

"A good way to keep hypothermia at bay."

"Besides this, it's what the beaver *does*—its behavior—that also helps. For instance, during the middle of winter, beavers avoid prolonged immersion by shortening the length of their underwater excursions. This means frequent short trips as opposed to a few long ones. They can warm up in between. The young kits are especially vulnerable to cooling, and their family dotes upon them heavily. Parents and older siblings will physically haul kits back into the lodge when a prudent time has elapsed."

Lost in my underwater imaginings I failed to notice that Randy's freehand was now aimed at the lodge. I looked at Alan. He pointed to his watch then briskly raised two fingers. Right. Time to check out the lodge.

"How cold do you figure it is in this lodge right now?" Randy said as we both turned around to confront it.

"The coldest recorded temperature inside an occupied northern lodge is minus four, quite balmy really, considering that, when this measurement was taken, it was minus forty-five outside. A typical family of around five animals provides central heating for the lodge. Their body heat keeps it around four to six degrees above zero for most of the winter." I clambered up the side of the lodge. "Come on up, Randy. It'll hold you." Alan let out a kilometer of slack on the microphone cord, allowing Randy to climb untethered to the roof of the lodge. "This little home is well insulated from extreme cold and icy winds, and it's virtually impregnable to predators. A bear, wolf or wolverine might try to hack their way in. But this thing's a fortress. Even if they did get through all these sticks and frozen mud, the beavers would be long gone, down the plunge hole, leaving behind only a trail of bubbles to snap at."

With some consternation I noticed that Alan's right index finger was now pointed upwards, making swift circles through the air. Randy saw it too. "Before we go," said Randy, "you claimed earlier that we might be able to hear beaver activities in this lodge. Can we listen in?"

"First we have to find the air vent."

"The air vent?"

"Yes, the air vent. All occupied lodges have them. Imagine how stuffy it would get in there without one." I pulled the garden trowel out of my parka pocket and started probing gently through the snow and sticks at the top of the lodge. "Ah, here it is. If it was dead calm and the morning sun was shining on the lodge, we would see plumes of beavers' breath wafting out of this vent. When they're slapping all that mud on the inside walls in the fall—it's just like adobe—they always leave an open spot directly on top. My hope is that we can sneak that fancy mike of yours down this hole and listen in."

"I'm game, Jamie. What do you expect to hear?"

"I don't know exactly. They have a rather narrow vocabulary. Most beaver linguists, of which there are few, recognize three main groups of sounds: the whine, the grunt and the hiss. The little ones tend to whine a lot when begging for food or a grooming session. We're a bit early for the mating season. They may respond aggressively to your mike. Who knows what we'll hear, if anything." Alan in the meantime was cutting his throat with his thumb. "Be careful, Randy. I don't want to be too intrusive." I carefully widened an orifice through the sticks for the mike to slip through. "Okay, lower away, Randy." And down it went into the beaver's invisible world.

"Not too far, Randy. You don't want to drop it on them . . . or sink it down a plunge hole!" To our radio listeners, my voice sounded increasingly muffled as the microphone descended. We were shouting at each other. "Can you hear anything, Randy?"

"Nothing. . . . No, wait a minute. Listen to that!" I cranked the volume knob on my headset. From inside the lodge came high whimpering sounds followed by rhythmic thumps and low grunts.

"That's the funniest sounding beavers I've ever heard!" said Randy, laughing like a teenager. I had rarely seen him so animated. "What do you think they're doing?"

I had no answers. I think I was startled by our acoustical success. "As I said, I think it's too early for mating. They usually show no interest in these matters until early February. And they much prefer to do it in the water. But then again—"

Randy cut in with a loud "Uh-oh!" More thumps and grunts were transmitted live across the western Arctic. "There they go again. It sounds like a steamy wild romantic morning in there!" he exclaimed as the *Mackenzie Morning* sign-off jingle sounded in our headsets. Some engineer back in the studio's master control room apparently had decided that our broadcast time had expired.

"Maybe we should leave them in peace," said Randy as he started reeling in the mike cord.

I couldn't have agreed more. We had boldly crossed a frozen threshold between worlds. Yet I was suddenly struck by the need for some common courtesy between us up top and them below.

"Let's get that thing out of there!"

"We're out!" yelled Alan curtly as he started winding our long mike cord around his arm. Randy and I leaped respectfully off the top of the beaver lodge, then stuffed all our electronic paraphernalia into my big toboggan. Randy made himself a passable roost on a thick coil of wire and climbed in. Alan stood tall against the backboard, looking like a sled-musher ready to shout orders to his dogs. "We *just* made it under the wire that time boys," he said, reverting back to his boyish grinning self. As I revved my cold snowmobile a few times, I glanced back at the snow-caked lodge. I wondered what all our ruckus must have sounded like for the occupants within. I felt like shouting "Thanks" and "Good-bye." But perhaps by now the beavers were well out of earshot, chomping on cattail rootstocks or sucking back air bubbles hundreds of meters away. How could I tell? Like so much about life beneath the shroud of subarctic snow, there was much more going on down there than meets the eye.

DASHING THROUGH
THE SNOW

*Snow is considered excellent if the climber can stand
on or near the surface, only fair if he sinks to his calves;
when immersion is knee-deep or greater it is good only
for building character.*
—*Climbing Committee of the Mountaineers*

Lone youth. Middle-class male Caucasian. Just released from a stuffy high school classroom. With body slouched but head and shoulders up, he was mounted on a growling '97 Thundercat. Three-cylinder, high-performance Suzuki engine, 896cc, liquid cooled. "Two hundred kilometers an hour right out of the box," the salesman had promised. Rider and snow machine moved as one. He, it, crept slowly towards the frozen lakeshore going the wrong way down a one-way willow-edged lane. Double wishbone coil suspension over gas-filled shocks. "Permits precise handling and aggressive cornering over the roughest bumps and moguls." This was a hungry predator, a jungle cat stalking a wild boar, a polar bear approaching a seal hole, a wolverine shadowing a stranded caribou calf. "Undisputed world's fastest production snowmobile."

The immobile faceless head was shrouded in red plastic. The head was perched on top of a leather jacket totally black except for silver studs around each wrist and shoulder. Bright orange mitts of windproof Dacron wrapped like claws around the throttle and brake controls. This was a scavenger sniffing the air for the scent of dead meat, a snow vulture

complete with raw red head, somber dark body and flashing
talons. Lightweight plastic skis with carbide runners. "Less
friction in the snow for improved acceleration and top
speed." The head began turning jerkily from side to side as if
suddenly glimpsing or smelling its quarry. "Extended and
reinforced track promotes flotation over fresh snow."

A few meters from the lake the low growl rose to a raspy
snarl. The Thundercat lurched forward, then stopped abruptly as its master buttoned down his studded cuffs. A bluff.
Together the engine, power train, chassis and forty-two liters
of high octane gas ("for extended trail riding") weighed just
under 280 kilograms. In a lightening flash the growl rose to a
shrieking howl. No bluff. Visible to invisible in six seconds.
Inaudible in twenty-five. Rider and snow chariot disappeared
in a quivering plume of shattered snow crystals suspended in
the frigid windless air.

The rider became instantly intoxicated by the scream of
his engine, the rush of wind past his helmet and the tremendous G-forces. Adrenaline surged into the reptilian part of his
brain. Gasoline sprayed into the piston chambers and exploded. At eighty kilometers an hour, corrugated drifts on the lake
kept machine and rider in the air as much as on the snow. At
a hundred and twenty there were no bumps, just an unbroken hum beneath rider's well-padded seat. He crossed the
lake in three minutes flat. What then? Turn around and cross
it again, of course. This cycle repeated itself a few times until
a shadow of boredom stole into his mind. At the far side of
the lake the Thundercat idled for a moment as the rider
stepped off to urinate. As the snow yellowed, the faceless head
turned slowly toward shore. It spotted something. What? An
ancient ax blaze on a lakeside birch marked an overgrown
trail into the bush. Unhampered by forethought or reason,
the rider leaped back on his machine and thundered off into

the boreal forest. A startled raven launched from the top of a nearby veteran spruce tree, flinging its *who-haw* call at the intruder.

Acceleration was poor in the fresh loose snow. The Thundercat moved forward awkwardly in short whining bursts of speed. No one had been down this trail recently, perhaps not since the 1950s. It wound through a densely packed forest of young spruce, over treeless bedrock ridges and along the edge of sheltered ponds and creeks. These were not the usual hunting grounds of a Thundercat. The narrow trail was virtually blocked in some spots by thick alder shrubs, but the rider managed to power through them all, unvanquished.

Five kilometers inland, rider and machine sprang out of the crowded woods in a sudden rush of unbridled power and landed with a muffled thud on a small beaver pond. For a few rare moments the Thundercat did not move. Without daring to take his orange mitt from the throttle control, for therein lay his security, the rider rose up on his haunches and swung his head slowly over one shoulder then the other. The pond's steep-sided shore was rimmed entirely by an impregnable fence of young black spruce and tangled willows. The rider's shoulders made a rapid up and down movement. Without hesitating he did two 360-degree power spins on the ice, then bolted for the trail down which he had just come. Traveling was much easier on the way out thanks to the packing job he had done. The minor defeat the rider swallowed at the beaver pond was more than compensated by the thrill of screaming over huge moguls of muskeg at forty kilometers an hour— until he completely lost control at a sharp turn. Unseen by his buddies the rider plowed the world's fastest production snow machine into a gaping hollow of pristine meter-deep snow.

The Thundercat was swallowed whole. The rider tried to ease it out of the hole in low gear. The machine moved down but not forward. He whipped it into reverse. It sank some more. How about full throttle forward? A huge shower of snow and more sinking, that's all. Nothing on board could entice the snow to disgorge its victim. For the first time since leaving the high school parking lot, the rider took off his helmet. A freckled fifteen-year-old face appeared. Its limp expression revealed evidence of a badly bruised ego just below the surface. The gleaming red helmet slipped from his fingers into deep powder snow. He rubbed his temple with one hand and tugged at his red hair with the other. For the first time since lunch (when he chose a jelly donut over chocolate-covered), he began to think. As he stared woefully at the smoking tail of his father's beloved Thundercat poking out of the snow, it occurred to him that he would need more than wishbone coils to get himself out of this mess. Perhaps a 4x4 with a very long winch? Or maybe a helicopter with a sturdy sling? Too dazed for any more thinking, the boy turned his back on the scene of the accident and stumbled down the trail, leaving the Thundercat still growling beneath the snow. The exacting laws of locomotion over snow had claimed another victim.

Fifty years ago there lived a Russian ecologist named A.N. Formozov, who spent many long hours watching animals engaged in a life-and-death struggle with snow. From the snowfields of Siberia to the frosted slopes of the Ural Mountains he observed northern animals in the wild and concluded that snow poses one of the most profound environmental challenges they face. "Snow cover, for many species, is the most important element of environmental resistance," wrote Formozov, "and the struggle against this particular element is almost beyond some species' ability."

He carried this notion further by classifying animals according to their ability to cope with the demands imposed on them by snow. He recognized a spectrum of categories based on how well adapted to snow an animal may be. At one end, the maladapted end, was the chionophobe—from the Greek *chion*, "snow," and *phobe*, "fear"—snow haters you might say. (Can't handle a little wind? You'd be a pneuma-phobe and so on.) In this category he lumped small ungulates like his native steppe antelope, many sparrow-sized birds and small cats. Watch a house cat shake that hateful snow off its little paws and you'll know what a chionophobe is. At the other end of Formozov's snow spectrum were the chionophiles—*philos* being Greek for "dear" or "loving." The snow lovers. All species Formozov put in this category, which he affectionately called Chionees, lived in regions of "hard winters with much snow." These included such northern icons as the rock and willow ptarmigan, snowshoe hare, arctic fox and several species of lemmings.

Formozov built a number of gradations into his classification system, putting caribou, moose and wolves for instance somewhere near the middle. Foremost among his criteria for classifying a species as snow lover or hater or something in between was an ability to *move* through snow while searching for food, escaping from predators or generally just getting around. Sometimes deep and fluffy, sometimes hard and crusty, sometimes wet and mushy, snow in its many forms and phases presents a vast range of possibilities that may either help or hobble an animal engaged in the simple act of locomotion.

You may ask where we humans fit on this spectrum. On a good day in the bush, equipped with the right snow propulsion technology, you might be a chionophile. On a bad day, equipped with nothing but your running shoes and wearing snow to your knees, you're probably a chionophobe. To some people, many of them in their teens, the invention of the snowmobile represents the ultimate surrender of snow to our age-old struggle to move over it. Is this conquest not proven by the snowmobile's meteoric rise to popularity over the past few decades? What full-blooded, able-bodied, well-heeled northern bushman or woman does not own, or want to own, at least one snowmobile? What technology could possibly challenge this machine's role as the world's number one form of snow locomotion? A team of sled dogs for instance is too slow, too unreliable, too complicated and, let's face it, too noisy and smelly to be of much use nowadays, isn't it?

At least one native trapper from Alaska isn't so sure. He's keeping his options open just in case the snowmobile one day falls from grace. "Oh, I don't use my dogs hardly at all now, since I got a machine," he told anthropologist Richard Nelson. "But I always keep at least two dogs around anyway, just in case I need pups. We never know how long we'll have all this white man stuff, so we might need a dog team if there's no more machines."

If you're not interested in speed and can handle the downside of owning anywhere from two to twenty dogs, a team hitched to the right kind of sled represents the perfect vehicle for traversing snow. On the wind-hardened snow of the tundra, nothing surpasses the Inuit *komatik* for ease of pulling, lightness, ruggedness, plus economy of manufacture and maintenance. Its design is elegantly simple: a flat bed of wooden planks supported by raised double runners often rimmed with flexible low-friction strips of white Teflon. Instead of rigid nails or bolts, the classic *komatik* is held together with ropes that allow ample give and take while it pounds across the cement-like tundra snow. Before rope

Sled dogs ready to hit the taiga trail. (Photo: Tessa Macintosh)

arrived in the Arctic, caribou *babiche* held *komatiks* together. Before wooden planks it was whale bone and seal hides. And before Teflon, runners were often lined with frozen fish wrapped in skins—it's still a *komatik*. The dogs are hitched in a loose fan-shaped pattern that maximizes their pulling power while reducing their temptation to lunge for one another's throats, as sled dogs are wont to do.

Now take this marvelous invention south to the taiga forest, the land of little sticks and soft deep snow. It's next to useless. The *komatik*'s narrow sled runners will bog down, and your dogs will tie themselves in knots around the trees and one another. Much gnashing of teeth will follow, including your own. Don't try it. Leave the *komatik* where it belongs: on the tundra. What you need is a long narrow toboggan made of sturdy birch or oak boards with a tight snow-shedding curl up front. Outfit this with roped canvas sides, a sturdy backboard, wooden handles for the musher to hang onto and a team of dogs hitched in tandem. Sure, the dogs may fight a bit more than on a fan hitch, but consider the alternative. Actually, when taking dogs down narrow forest trails, there *is* no alternative. This time-tested technology is perfectly matched to the type of snow and terrain found throughout much of the subarctic. Try in vain to design a better motorless mode of snow locomotion with equal pulling power and cargo capacity.

Like the birchbark canoe the dog-powered woodland toboggan was a major player in getting Canada up and running as a country. Contrary to popular opinion it was actually thousands of panting, yelping, snapping sled dogs that knit our confederation together—not long-wigged barristers and bureaucrats. Dogs hauled countless tons of furs and mail and freight and supplies from fort to fort and post to post. And the wisdom embodied in the woodland toboggan's basic design, like the canoe's, has endured over the span of several centuries. May the snowmobile fare at least half as well.

For the snowy North the invention of the dog sled in its various regionally attuned forms represents a technological breakthrough in human locomotion. It stands at least on par with the invention of the large wooden-wheeled wagons still drawn throughout much of Asia by a horse, donkey, bullock or acquiescent human. But far more significant to northern history—more on par with the invention of the wheel—is the making of the world's first snowshoe.

Some historians mark the year 4,000 B.C. as the approximate birth date of the snowshoe, or more properly, "the first device to serve as a foot-extender for easier travel over snow." According to this school of thought, central Asian nomads came up with the idea, which they used to their advantage in migrating into northern Europe and Siberia. Musing on the extraordinary significance of this invention, an historian named Hatt proposed eighty years ago that the entire circumpolar world could be lumped into two discrete cultures based solely on their winter footgear. The oldest of these he called the Coast Culture. Because these people lacked snowshoes, they could not travel or hunt over the deep inland snows. In winter they were restricted to the shores of oceans, lakes or rivers, where they were forced to subsist mostly on fish. "The subsequent invention of the snowshoe in the Old World," writes Hatt, "and its diffusion in North America would have permitted a later 'Inland Culture' to occupy the entire length and breadth of the northern boreal forest, from Lapland to Labrador." Other historians argue that snowshoes were invented much earlier and would view Hatt's theory as clever bunk. They envision the first North Americans tromping east across the Bering Land bridge in primitive snowshoes around fourteen thousand years ago.

Such debate over dates has no relevance for the Chipewyan native people who live in the heart of Canada's subarctic. They are among the many northern cultures who owe their very existence to the snowshoe. Accordingly, in a story called "The First Man," they push the creation of snowshoes back beyond the reach of any clock or calendar to the very dawn of earthly time.

"In the beginning," goes the Chipewyan tale, "man did not exist. Then suddenly there was man, it is said. Who made man? We do not know. When winter came, man made himself some snowshoes." This did not come quickly or easily to man, having little if any woodworking experience. "How am I going to do it?" he wondered. Guided mostly by the seat of his caribou-skin pants, he cut down a birch tree, managed to build a passable frame, installed the crossbars, then brought the project to a halt. "How will I do the latticework?" he thought, for he had no woman to do it for him, as was the custom in those earliest of days. He lay down for a long winter's nap, and when he awoke he saw that his snowshoe frames had been partially laced. "Who could have laced my snowshoes while I was asleep?" he said to himself, for he was quite alone. This construction by magical increments went on for several nights to the mounting puzzlement of man. Then one morning, just as he was waking up, he saw a ptarmigan flying up through the hole in the roof of his tepee. "Aha! It must have been the ptarmigan!" he exclaimed.

Again the next night he went to sleep and at daybreak, through shifty, half-closed eyes, he glimpsed the ptarmigan flying up and away. He looked at his snowshoes. They were almost completely laced. "Hmmm, I know just what to do," he said to himself. That evening he covered the top of his tepee with the skin of a black bear. Then he lay down to sleep, smiling to himself.

When man woke the next morning, his finished snowshoes were lying beside him. There in the shadows was the ptarmigan. It looked cautiously at man, startled to see him awake so early. "I must fly away quickly," she thought, but when she fluttered up to the tent roof she discovered that her escape route was blocked. She dropped in defeat to the tepee floor and turned instantly into a beautiful woman with long silky hair. As the story goes, "the man and the woman slept together, of course, and in time they had many children. We are their descendants."

The exact shape and size of those primeval snowshoes is left a mystery. No doubt ptarmigan woman had the local snow conditions in mind when she designed them. Most of the traits peculiar to traditional snowshoe styles used by native people across northern North America have everything to do with variations in snow. The shape and angle of the toe, the tightness and pattern of the lacework, the number of crossbars, the presence or absence of a toe hole, the

Snowshoes can take you where you want to go, even help you build a home. These girls built their quinzhee snow shelter using snowshoes as shovels. (PHOTO: TESSA MACINTOSH)

overall width and length, the total surface area of the frame—all these features vary from region to region in concert with the prevailing density, depth, weight and moisture content of snow. For instance in the central subarctic of the Northwest Territories, where some of the continent's lightest, driest and fluffiest snow falls, traditional Dene snowshoes are typically long and narrow for maximum stability and speed. They have sharply upturned toes, making it next to impossible to catch the tips in deep snow. They are laced with a tight hexagonal weave for maximum flotation. To the east, where the snow is deeper and heavier, the Cree favor the huge round beavertail design that can measure half a meter in diameter. It incorporates a very fine *babiche* mesh into which the elders often weave images of guardian spirits to boost hunting success on the trail. And to the west from Alaska come perhaps the biggest snowshoes ever made, so-called whales, designed for the deep mushy snow found on the southern slopes of the Alaska Range. These monsters include several crossbars, sharply upturned toes and a tip-to-tail length well over two meters. Says one devoted whale user, "They're not fast but boy do they float!"

Crouched, silent and still, on the evolutionary summit of animal adaptations to snow is *Lepus americanus*, the snowshoe hare. This species' solution to the problem of locomotion in a snow-dominated landscape is a pair of enormous paws that act, as its common name suggests, exactly like snowshoes. They are covered in long stiff hairs that almost double the flesh-and-bone foot within. This design permits nimble passage over the softest, deepest snow, in which the hare's predator's often flounder. More than providing traction, the hare's marvelous feet provide impressive speed. Down a semipacked trail, a snowshoe hare can vault along at over forty kilometers an hour, covering as much as three meters in a single bound.

The snowshoe hare literally floats over snow. So does its chief predator, the lynx, which relies on nearly circular, well-furred paws that are huge in proportion to the rest of its body. From the perspective of diet, the body of a lynx consists mainly of reconstituted snowshoe hare. As naturalist Ernest Thompson Seton remarked, "The lynx lives on rabbits, follows the rabbits, thinks rabbits, tastes like rabbits, increases with them, and on their failure, dies of starvation in the unrabbited woods." As good a "rabbit" hunter as the lynx is (hares and true rabbits are physically quite distinct), its chances of winter survival are very much at the mercy of snow conditions. Weighing up to ten times more than a hare, a lynx must stalk undetected to within a few bounds of its prey or risk bogging down during the heat of pursuit. One long-term field study in northern Alberta showed that at the best of times, when the snow was settled and firm, the odds of a lynx chasing down and snatching a hare off its feet were one in four. When the snow was particularly soft, with little bearing strength, the lynx's odds of making a successful kill plummeted to less than one in ten. More precisely, in ninety-one chases out of a hundred, the hare got away. With a good fluff to the snow, its jumbo feet nearly always prevailed over the lynx's hunger.

It would be a travesty to the laws of ecology if these two animals were equally gifted floaters. If the odds of capture became too favorable, the north woods would soon be both unrabbited and unlynxed. By calculating an animal's "weight load," biologists can accurately portray how easily it negotiates passage over snow. This index measures an animal's body weight in relation to the area of its feet in contact with the snow. The smaller the weight load—measured in grams per square centimeter—the better the floater.

Most northern lynx weigh in the neighborhood of eight to ten kilograms. Factor in the area covered by its sizable paws and you get a weight load index of 34 gm/cm^2. For comparison, most common house cats have a weight load of about 100 gm/cm^2. They're definite sinkers. Although a snowshoe hare might weigh as much as a well-fed house cat—around 1.5 kilograms—its huge feet give it a weight load of barely 12 gm/cm^2—almost ten times better than a cat and three times better than a lynx.

How do humans measure up on the weight load scale? As fond as a I am of snow, I, for one, proceed through it more like a cat than a hare. My feather-weight daughters cheerfully pride themselves in strolling unperturbed over the surface of deep, crusty snow as I flounder beside them buried to my thighs. With my narrow, size twelve feet and a body weight of about eight-five kilograms, my weight load comes to 125 gm/cm^2. To float over fluffy snow as efficiently as a snowshoe hare, I would need at least a size 120 shoe. Not very serviceable in the jumbled north woods.

Technology allows us to sprout wings and streak across the sky like a peregrine falcon, to acquire fins and plumb the ocean depths like a bowhead whale. This we can do with apparent precision and ease. Similarly, to traverse the fluffy frontier of subarctic snow with the field-tested reliability of a snowshoe hare we must again turn to technology to supplement the meager propulsion of our unremarkable feet. In this domain, we are led to believe, the evolutionary summit is staunchly held by none other than the snowmobile.

Faster, smoother, higher over the snow. Year after year, this is where the snowmobile industry vows to take us. The fact that these machines are now being churned out in colors varying from neon green to shocking pink serves to boost their image of invincibility and float them seductively to the surface of the consumer's restless mind. Just how much farther this technology can take us—beyond mere paint and power upgrades—remains to be seen. In spite of the great strides in the art and science of building a better snowmobile, could it be that we already have reached an evolutionary threshold beyond which the snowy frontier will not yield?

I was an ardent chionophile when I unlashed my snowshoes to climb aboard my first snowmobile. But I quickly discovered that it was a real sinker. A deadweight. A definite loser in deep snow. All motor and no track. Absolutely every time I moved it, I found myself wondering what a hernia felt like. What did I know about snowmobiles ten years ago? Nothing. We bonded quickly, that snowmobile and me. High comfy seat for my long legs, elevated windscreen to shield my tall frame. I especially liked its orange hood with big black stripes down the side. The paint job reminded me of the orange and black canoes I used to paddle around Algonquin Park as a kid. My camp colors. I bought the snowmobile off a friend who had to leave town in a hurry. It was a good deal though rather fast. He showed me how to change the spark plugs, mix the oil and grease the bogey wheels that kept the track from flying off at high speeds.

"You may not need the speed, but the extra power comes in handy," he said. As we shook hands he added, "Make sure you keep up some speed if you hit deep snow. Whatever you do, don't stop."

The winter of my first snowmobile happened to be one of the snowiest in years. Though heeding my friend's advice as best I could, I did make many stops in deep snow, all of them unscheduled. At the controls of that machine I was an extreme chionophobe. My company, at least while I was driving that thing, became something of a liability to my fellow travelers. I learned early that the safest place for me to travel was in the rear. Let the other snowmobiles break trail. I would follow behind, sticking to their firm paths like a locomotive sticks to rails.

On one caribou hunting trip, while bringing up the rear as usual, I noticed the two machines in front of me suddenly starting to bob oddly. Their tails were going up and down like the back end of a jittery sandpiper. The driver just ahead of me twisted around abruptly and waved his free arm to get my attention. "What is it?" I yelled over the roar of my massive engine. He pointed to the trail behind his machine, made a slashing motion across his throat, then yelled back to me the dreaded "O" word: overflow!

Please, not overflow. I had seen it once before. Deep snow over a carpet of machine-eating slush. It usually occurs in winters with lots of heavy snow. All that extra weight presses down on the lake ice, often bending it to the cracking point. Water gushes up through the cracks to relieve pressure and saturates the bottom layers of snow. Deep snow above insulates the resulting slush from freezing. And there it lurks. Unpredictable. Undetectable. Invisible. Until torn open by some hapless snowmobiler.

With my thumb steady on the throttle, time slowed to a crawl, burdened by my ponderous thoughts. Dreaded overflow. If you are unlucky enough to sink into it, traction becomes impossible. It's like trying to drive over a mirror covered in a thick slurry of yesterday's porridge. You rev your engine. The track spins. The slush flies. You don't move. Besides getting miserably stuck the other mortal hazard is getting your machine and yourself inextricably frozen into the open wound of slush. As soon as the overflow is exposed to the cold air, everything begins to freeze. It is an insidious process. You first notice it when large blobs of frozen slush start sticking to your machine's track. Then its skis. Then you look down at your boots! They've doubled in size, having become coated with ice balls while you sloshed around in that blue-gray muck. You dig and spin, dig and spin, curse and dig. You go nowhere fast.

Such images raced through my mind as I drove headlong into a dilemma. The choice was dreadfully simple: stop or go. Beneath my three layers of mitts (it was minus thirty) my knuckles must have gone white. So did my face, I imagine. The trail in front of me was turning gray. I chose go. Without daring to slow down I cruised with pseudo-confidence toward the spot in question. I had to keep moving. "Whatever you do, don't stop. . . ."

My friends got through okay. Floated right over the stuff, no problem. They were on the other side now. Both had jumped off their machines to get a good look at me coming straight at them. They knew all about my machine. Twice today already they'd helped dig me out of the snow.

Several winters ago one driver walked away from a snow-mobile stuck in overflow and never came back. After trying for hours to get the thing out, he finally gave up in frustration, consigning his machine to a springtime trip to the bottom of the lake. "Good riddance," he said as he grabbed his pack and began the long march back to town.

I should have done that when I got stuck. Let it sink I mean. To the bottom of the lake. Good-bye. Forever and ever. Amen. My machine was, after all, well insured. Instead we spent the rest of the afternoon digging and spinning and cursing until we finally got it out. We were of course sopping wet as much from sweat as from slush. What followed was, I swear, the biggest campfire I have ever seen. The three of us stood round that fire, drying our socks, guffawing at my mis-fortune, sipping hot cider and eating leftover rum balls and Christmas cake. My orange and black ice-encrusted snow-mobile sat safely, high and dry, out on the wind-packed snow in the middle of the bay.

My next snowmobile was the flip side of my first. Virtually no motor and all track. "A long-track," the salesman told me. "Its previous owner was a trapper from Snare Lakes. Lots of deep powder up there, you know. He broke a lot of trail with this here machine. He likes the long-track so much he buys

a new one each year." Just what I need, I thought, as the salesman rang up the cash register. A real floater. Unsinkable. A
deep-powder *Titanic*.

Float it did. Wonderfully. No snow was too deep for my
long-track. Nothing could stop me now. I actually came to
enjoy the experience of snowmobiling . . . most of the time.
Until the day I got stuck in overflow again. It happened on a
U-shaped lake a few kilometers behind my wilderness cabin.
Horseshoe Lake we call it. My new machine and I were
packing a trail across the lake for the next day's ski trip when
I impulsively got it into my head that it would be smart to
make a loop trail right around the lake. My, this *is* deep, I
thought as I plowed into a huge drift near the lakeshore. I felt
like I was skippering a boat through deep swells of water. It
was fun while it lasted. As it turned out I *was* on water and
sinking fast. I sliced into some slush that was too thick and
too soupy to support even my mighty long-track.

My wife, Brenda, knew I was still alive when she heard my
loud barking grunts. My ten-minute spin to pack trails had
turned into a two-hour wrestling match to get my machine
unstuck. I had kept the engine running all that time, figuring
that its warmth might postpone the inevitable freezing
process. In the dead calm air a stinking cloud of blue smoke
hung over the scene of the accident. The temperature, like the
sun, was dropping fast. Brenda stopped briefly to assess both
the condition of the snow and my mood, then marched
bravely into the overflow. She had brought a shovel and we
dug and spun together for a while in the slush.

"This is pointless!" she announced after her third and my
thirtieth attempt to drive the machine onto safe snow. "Did
you bring an ax?" she asked. "No," I said in a slurred voice,
"but I have a collapsible saw in the glove box."

"Good," she said snatching it from my shaking, frozen

mitt. "Have you eaten anything lately? You're sounding hypothermic."

It slowly dawned on me that I had eaten nothing since breakfast. "Not much," I said. "Shall we order out for pizza?"

Half an hour and several spruce trees later we had engineered a large round platform made out of logs. About two meters in diameter, it sat on top of some fresh snow above the plunge hole, where my stinking long-track now gurgled in the thickening slush. I glanced up through the smoke to see the night's first stars twinkling merrily at us. Time was running out. My gas gauge read empty. Everything was freezing, including my brain. "It's now or never," said Brenda as she jumped back into the slush. I took the front and she took the back and we lifted that snow machine out of the hole and set it gingerly upon the log mat. It held. It floated. Although we knew there was overflow below, the machine was now free and clear of danger. I put my wet slushy arm around Brenda and said, "You're brilliant! A snowshoe for a snowmobile." An ancient idea come to the rescue of modern technology.

The next morning we returned with real snowshoes and a can of gas. In front of the perched machine we stomped a trail leading well away from the disaster area. We filled the gas tank, chipped frozen slush off the track, then abandoned the machine for a second time. Another cold night gave our little snow road the consistency of concrete. Two days after driving into the overflow, I started up my trusty long-track, inched carefully off the log mat, then roared down the trail. My snow-loving wife, who takes no chances, chose to snowshoe back to the cabin.

BILL MAC

He knew his fish and liked to fish. He knew the plants, animals and birds of the region. He became a veritable encyclopedia of geological information. He had tremendously broad interests.
—John Parker, Commissioner of the Northwest Territories, 1982

Your house is on fire. You're running out the door. What do you grab? Your wallet? A treasured painting? Photo albums? Your favorite chair? Not Bill Mac. He grabbed his cigar boxes. Dozens of them. Even while flames leapt toward his cabin door, he dashed in again and again, scooping them off a high plywood shelf, now obscured by smoke. Back outside he lay them gently, one by one, on a cushion of thick grass near the lakeshore. Just a few more loads and that should do her, thought Bill, and in he went again.

Probably no one heard his muffled yell when the flames finally got to his bare hands. Everyone had run to get buckets. A neighbor just arriving on the scene saw Bill emerge from his cabin for the last time, with cigar boxes piled high on his outstretched arms and second degree burns on his hands.

The smell and sight of woodsmoke on such a hot still night as this caught the scattered residents of Jolliffe Island off guard. They knew it could mean only one thing. Converging on the smoke from all directions, a handful of prospectors, miners and woodcutters with buckets in hand crashed down the spruce-lined trails that led to Bill's cabin. By the time the fire brigade arrived from the mainland, Bill was already at the hospital having his hands wrapped in cotton gauze. The men quickly snuffed out all traces of flames with their makeshift water pumps and help from the island's volunteer bucket brigade.

Though it was approaching midnight, lively chatter drifted from most of the island's cabins, shacks and tents. As the coffee poured and neighbor congratulated neighbor, Bill's home burst again into flames with much greater violence than before. The fire brigade returned, this time with a good-sized fire hose in their boat. But it was too late. Bill's cabin and everything in it blazed into oblivion.

News travels fast in an isolated frontier mining town. The story made the front page of the Yellowknife paper. It sat below a hand-drawn *News of the North* flagstaff and the date July 10, 1953. The headline: "Fire Takes Valued Collections."

The Jolliffe Island residence of W.L. "Bill" McDonald, well known authority on many phases of northern life was completely destroyed by a double outbreak of fire on Tuesday night. With the house went valuable collections of birds eggs, along with collections of historical and archaeological interest. [They included] Mr. McDonald's books, copies of his many reports on the geology and natural history of the north and other priceless memoranda of a busy life spent in the Territories.

No one knows for sure just how many of Bill's precious eggs were consumed by the flames. He managed to save a few hundred of them in those carefully piled cigar boxes. Among the other memoranda destroyed was a huge bookcase of well-preserved and well-read first edition volumes about arc-

Part of Bill's collection of raptor and duck eggs salvaged from the 1953 fire. They were packed in one of his original cigar boxes padded with stupendously soft goose down. (PHOTO: BOB BROMLEY)

tic explorers—one of the best collections in the country lost to future generations.

In 1892 James S. McDonald toted some of those explorers' books across the Atlantic from his Isle of Skye home. By the turn of the century, his seven-year-old son William was reading them most evenings once all the chores were done on their ranch near Camrose Alberta.

"I'd read quite a bit on explorers long before I came north," Bill told CBC Radio in a 1971 series called *Voice of the Pioneers*. "Quite often, some of the Mounties that had spent time down the Mackenzie used to come and stay with us. And they would tell stories about the north too. Well, I think that was the thing that started me. I wanted to see the north afterwards."

The long road Bill took to get there was paved with reflective candlelight readings, intensive study and the scholarship gained from many years of watching and working the land. Bill's favorite teacher was the rolling aspen parkland encircling their ranch. Besides ranch work his curriculum included fishing for pickerel along Driedmeat Creek, hunting pintails and mallards beside potholes and sloughs, calling to coyotes at night round a campfire and gazing up in wonder at the great Vs of snow geese winging their way north each spring.

Bill took formal schooling seriously when he had to. On New Year's Day, 1913, at age nineteen, he resolved to go to university. But several years of full-time ranching, railway work and carpentry left him way short on required courses. No problem, thought Bill. He came indoors and rolled up his sleeves. "From the first of the year till the first of May I studied and memorized everything I could, and I wrote the McGill matric on the first of May." Having digested three years of high school in four months, Bill passed the exam. That September the University of Alberta in Edmonton opened its doors for the sixth time. On the registrar's list of a few dozen students was one William Leslie McDonald.

Just as he was gathering a good head of academic steam, his studies were chopped by overseas trench duty during the war. But he returned with renewed gusto four years later to focus on geology and mining engineering. This program offered many field opportunities though it was not always rocks Bill went looking for. A fellow classmate, Frank Moyle, remembers one outing with Bill down the Bow River near Banff. Bill was bagging bugs, aquatic insects for the University collection.

"He took me on my first canoe trip and, as we paddled along, he pointed out the many aspects of nature which I, as a young boy, had never been aware of. The interest and respect for our land and its inhabitants which he instilled in

Bill had a special fondness for raptorial birds, including this imma-ture northern goshawk, which he encountered during one his many field expeditions. (PHOTO: HENRY BUSSE)

me that evening has enriched my life and is with me still." Behind Frank was a man who sat tall in the stern, sweeping the water with slow self-assured strokes. He was barefoot, wearing khaki pants, a faded green high-necked Windbreaker and a stout visored cap. From the left corner of his mouth hung a stubby Cuban cigar. His eyes were cool but gentle and

rimmed with smile lines. Rarely did those eyes hold a person
in their gaze for very long, especially outside, for they, like his
big-lobed ears, were always tuned to the subtle motions and
expressions that danced across nature's face.

The call north came in 1920. The Imperial Oil Company
hired Bill, still a student, to haul equipment, drill holes and
shoulder rock samples up and down the south shore of Great
Slave Lake. He came back for more the next summer and the
next. Bill fast became an expert expediter for northern surveys. Recognizing Bill's reliability and renown as a field man,
the Consolidated Mining & Smelting Company snapped him
up as leader of its Northern Exploration Team. It was part of
an aggressive campaign of geological and geographical exploration of the unknown parts of northern Canada covering
about eighty thousand square kilometers in the area surrounding Athabasca and Great Slave Lake. Bill's early dreams
of northern exploration were being more than fulfilled.

That summer the team's main target zone embraced the
south and east shores of Great Slave. He knew just what to
purchase for such a trip. Among the myriad items on his shop-
ping list were a few bars of Royal Crown toilet soap, small
plugs of McDonald tobacco (no relation), several boxes of
"Eddie Stinker" matches, a few colored bandanna handker-
chiefs (red and blue flowered) and a kilogram of tallow to fix
the canoes in case of an accident. Hob-nailed boots were
definitely not on Bill's list: tallow or no, they tended to ruin
canoes from the inside out. Bill was on friendly terms with
most of the provisioners in Edmonton, and he knew well how
to bargain with them. But he knew not where to find decent
maps of their route, concluding finally that they did not exist.

"It came as a bit of a shock to all of us that the government maps were just outlines of major lakes and rivers,"
wrote Bill's closest field partner, Ted Nagle, in *Prospector North*

of Sixty. "In 1926, there were of course no aerial survey maps. Once we left the well traveled routes we would be mapping our own trails."

It would not be Bill's first time navigating through a virtually unmapped landscape. Shrewd orienteering, paddling at night and the crossing of fingers—in that order—were Bill's tried and true means for getting his two Chestnut canoes and crew of five men safely across the oceanic stretches of Great Slave Lake. He filled his field books with finely penciled maps showing island after jagged island along the length of the lake's more sheltered east arm. On one of those islands a very curious Bill Dean once returned to camp holding a long straight branch which he had found stuck in the ground near the shore. He figured it was some kind of signpost. Two matches dangled from strings tied to its tip. Below them was a steel-nosed bullet tied around the branch. Bill knew immediately what it was. In those days natives of this region traveled between successive pots of tea. They used just one match to light a fire, so, Bill surmised, two matches meant two teas' distance. To him, the whole message was straightforward: good hunting two teas from this camp.

However well provisioned, Bill and his crew were compelled to hunt. Without extra fish and game they might have starved like some of those early explorers whose journals never got published. Toward the end of their expedition they could not let a single day go by without a successful hunt. Bill's sharp eye proved itself again and again behind the long barrel of his .22 Remington. Even with his eye trained on dinner the naturalist in Bill shone through.

"If a flock of birds flew over us he pointed out and named each species in it, then shot the finest eating ones out of the air," wrote Nagle, who never saw him waste any game.

On one raw day, while they canoe-sailed back toward Fort

Resolution, Bill's concentration held up even against the high winds and waves of late August. Again no one went hungry that night as Nagle remembers it: "With the leg-of-mutton sails raised, we flew across the whitecaps. The speed and exhilaration of that day struck a chord in all of us. While the rest of us ki-yied like wild men, McDonald stood in the bow of his canoe shooting ducks out of the air as we sped west. It was a thrilling day!"

Whether in the field of nuclear physics or frontier geology, great leaps forward along the path of knowledge often come right out of the blue to those who deserve it. So it was on that lucky April Fool's Day, 1936, just after Bill made camp on the west shore of Yellowknife Bay. Two of his men stumbled on some promising quartz samples while hacking a trail through the bush to their claim site. When they showed them to Bill, his eyes opened wide.

"What I saw was good. Damn good. When I found that first vein, I brought the drill. The heavy drill broke the snow and showed the rock. Right there, at that first vein oh, it just splashed with visible gold." Northern Canada's largest gold producer, the great Con Mine, rose from that very spot.

Not all of Bill's discoveries were so easily won. An unusual sparkle in the rocks along the south shore of Great Slave Lake had fired the imagination of prospectors for over thirty years: flashes of galena, a chunky ore commonly rich in silver, lead and zinc. Local natives used to smelt it down to make bullets and lead sinkers. They eventually led the rock people, as they called all visitors, to a concentrated outcrop near Pine Point. Over the years claims were staked on this site, then lapsed, staked, then lapsed again. Several waves of prospectors failed to find anything resembling a mother lode. On a hot muggy morning in August 1927, Bill decided to look one last time at the deposit.

He and Ted Nagle set off down an indistinct trail that promptly disappeared into a tangle of young jack pines and a labyrinth of fire-charred deadfall. Drought and high winds had dried up all the muskeg that summer and after six hours of tromping, they were thoroughly parched.

"My tongue was so dry and swollen," says Nagle, "that it felt like a big piece of cotton in my mouth. I could hardly speak."

Some mental relief came when they finally broke into a clearing and discovered a picked-over outcrop, a crude log cabin, a small mining shaft, but no water. There was only one thing to do, thought Bill in the fading light: trust the rotting beams and rickety ladder leading down that shaft and look for ice at the bottom. He discovered lots of lip-smacking ice, but sulfur leaching from the shaft walls had stained it a dirty stinky yellow. Melted and filtered through canvas and campfire charcoal, the water was just barely fit to drink as tea.

Further misadventures awaited them from sunset onward. Judging the cabin floor too filthy to sleep on, they bedded down beside the fire. In Nagle's memory that was one of the most miserable nights a man could spend in the bush.

"Soon after midnight it began to rain. Of course, we did not wake up until our bedding was soaked through. Then we lay awake, stifled beneath our wet blankets, listening to the mosquitoes humming above us."

The next day they were harassed by forest fires, tormented by flies and robbed by scavenging gray jays. But they got their ore samples—sixteen kilograms worth. So high was the ore grade that Consolidated Mining & Smelting executives in Edmonton began immediate plans for a full-scale lead-zinc mine. They would call it Pine Point.

"I was over there when they turned the power on," remembers Bill, "and to see them, with twenty-ton capacity

A man of ceaseless curiosity and deep affection for nature, Bill gently befriends a young bald eagle. (PHOTO: HENRY BUSSE)

trucks driving in and loading up and taking the stuff to a crusher and straight into the railway cars. Right then, that was one of the big things, since I had been on Pine Point right at the start."

Bill's knack for sniffing out precious minerals grew out of his boyhood curiosity and affection for wild country. He wanted to do a biology degree at the University of Alberta, but they didn't offer it in those days. So he went for the next best thing: rocks. "He was first and foremost a naturalist," says Dr. Bob Bromley, a Yellowknife ornithologist and former field apprentice of Bill's. His University of Alberta colleagues knew this and were thrilled to have one of their boys roving the uncharted northland. They wondered if he would be so kind as to send them specimens collected from his many expeditions. So did the Ottawa Museum. So did the U.S. Fish and Wildlife Service, the American Audubon Society and the Museum of Natural History in New York. So did the government scientists he met at the trading posts and Yellowknife cafés. Botanists, zoologists, ornithologists, entomologists, geologists. "They used to keep at me all the time. Keep notes on everything you see wherever you travel. They wanted me to try and collect so and so and so and so for them." Bill naturally complied and soon became a large diameter pipeline of scientific information flowing south. Collecting wild birds' eggs was a particular challenge for a man paid to carry rocks in his pack. It became one of Bill's passions.

LAPLAND LONGSPUR
Muskox Lake, June 15, 1945
   Nest in tundra hummock, lined with cotton grass and feathers.
   5 eggs, dusty brown and faintly mottled.

COMMON RAVEN
Yellowknife, April 20, 1948
   Stick nest on cliff face. Lined with caribou hair and shredded bark.
   8 bluish green eggs variously blotched and spotted with brown.

Bill McDonald's ever-present terrier strikes an unruffled pose beside a fledgling bald eagle during a visit to the West Mirage Islands on Great Slave Lake. (PHOTO: HENRY BUSSE)

Bill discovered birds that other people had spent years looking for. "In the early days there was very little known as to the nesting places of many of these birds that went north." Take the greater scaup for instance, black and white waterfowl emblem of the subarctic. "When the U.S. Wildlife people started coming in, they found that during the migration they'd see a few of the greater scaup on the lakes inland, along the road, but they'd never found any of them nesting. I took them out to the islands there, and we found something like fifty nests in two days."

Bill was a bird-banding pioneer. An arctic tern he banded on Great Slave Lake was picked up two years later near Durban, South Africa. A dark-eyed junco he banded near his cabin returned six years in succession until a cat swallowed most of it, though not the band, in Yellowknife's Old Town.

When once asked which was his favorite mineral, Bill chuckled and said, "I would say they're all about equal." He looked upon birds with similar equanimity but admitted a special fondness for bald eagles. He loved to go "down the bay"—Yellowknife Bay—whenever he could to watch the eagles around their nests, band any developing chicks and observe their progress toward that first solo flight.

Besides regularly reporting his observations to eager ornithologists down south, he once applied his eagle lore to the business of changing hearts. One spring a couple of boys, each carrying a rifle, were beating the bushes near his Jolliffe Island cabin. Bill figured they were "out to kill anything that moved," recounts historian Ray Price, so he invited them along on an eagle expedition down the bay. "The lads were so eager to go that they could hardly wait to get permission from their parents. Bill knew exactly where to find the eagles and knew they could come close to them. He let the boys watch as he fed the adult birds with fish. One of the eagles came so near they could have reached out and touched it. The boys were fascinated." On that spring day, they discovered what Price calls "the friendliness of the wild things."

Bill had a regular procession of children wandering across to his cabin. They often came to see his snowshoe hare. "That rabbit was a friend of mine," Bill told Price. "It used to come

Much to the amusement of his youthful audience, Bill wooed this snowshoe hare right out of the woods by his Jolliffe Island cabin. (PHOTO: HENRY BUSSE)

when I called it. The children heard about this and came across the Bay to see the performance. I let them stand at the window while I went outside and called it. They could scarcely believe their eyes when they saw the rabbit come, hop, hop, hop, out of the bush. On one occasion a local photographer came down to see this rabbit and take pictures. This time the rabbit not only came when it was called but jumped right into my arms."

In spite of his many field trips Bill alone could not have created such a well-worn path to his cabin door. He was in Price's words, "a man respected by all and consulted by many." At the height of the field season as many as a dozen prospectors a day came to see him, their packsacks loaded with freshly chipped rocks for him to examine. Among them were store clerks, taxi drivers and the owner of the Wildcat Café. As far as Bill could tell, "Everybody wanted to gamble on mining stock."

His former classmate and occasional field partner Frank Moyle called Bill "every prospector's friend. He never refused a request to examine and write a report on their prospects. How much was he paid? Like the old-time general practitioner, he was always on call—and as often was paid with 'Thanks.'"

"I don't know more than anybody," Bill would say to his departing visitors. "I've just traveled more."

Alone in his darkening cabin, Bill shoves his rock samples into a canvas sack, lights a kerosene lamp and pulls a large cardboard cigar box off a high shelf, "high enough so the kids can't get at it." Inside are today's field treasures: two peregrine falcon eggs nested tenderly in a thick layer of dark brown stupendously soft goose down. Bill slowly cups an egg into his hand and inspects its immaculate surface. About the size and shape of a small chicken egg, this one is creamy pink with faint streaks and misty dots all purplish brown. Circling its broader end is a wreath of bold scrawls resembling cryptic Neolithic cave paintings or Chinese calligraphy.

While still cradling the peregrine egg (called a duck hawk in those days) he reaches for a smaller cigar box. This one is made out of rough-hewn mahogany and latched shut with a small brass nail. Stamped on top are two swaying palm trees and a fringe of tobacco leaves surrounding a golden key. Inside are the tools of an egg blower. All carved into place in sturdy blue Styrofoam, Bill's array of silver alloy instruments could be mistaken as a dental kit for field mice. Tiny tweezers, picks, a fine-toothed file, a pair of finger-twist drills and a long tapered J-shaped tube.

Bill deftly pricks a minuscule hole on the egg's side. He inserts the flared drill head into the hole and gives it a few precise spins between his thumb and forefinger. *Rasp, rasp, rasp.* "That should do her," he mutters to himself. Two short pricks through the hole break the embryonic membrane inside. One egg ready for blowing. With the hole downward and over a bowl, Bill inserts the narrow tip of the J-shaped tube into the egg. Pinching his lips over the other end, he releases tight forceful puffs—like a trumpet player reaching for high C—until the last dribble of egg contents plops into the bowl. The other egg gets the same careful treatment. He washes his instruments in a basin of lake water, cranks up the flame on his lamp, then sets down to write.

DUCK HAWK
Yellowknife, June 14, 1943
    Nest on rock cliff in small cave. No nesting material.
    5 eggs, 2/3 incubated.

Thirty years later in a biology lab at the University of Alberta, those same peregrine eggs would be measured for shell thickness and strength. They would be mechanically fractionated and chemically decomposed. All this scrutiny to find out what peregrine eggs were like in a world not yet tainted by DDT and a host of other toxic pesticides that weakened their shells and pushed this species close to the brink of extinction.

Bill takes one last fond look at the peregrine eggs, gently lowers the cigar box lid and blows out the lamp.

However charming, Bill's egg collection deserved better than those cigar box nests. When curators at Yellowknife's Prince of Wales Northern Heritage Center received the collection, they deemed the cigar boxes unstable, unsound and generally unfit to protect such scientific treasures. Cardboard, whether Cuban or otherwise, contains slow release acids which could weaken the eggshells and sap them of color. One good jostle of a cigar box and the eggs could roll and bump and crack together. This clearly would not do.

"EGGS!! PLEASE, PLEASE HANDLE WITH CARE!! PLEASE LEAVE EGGS EXACTLY IN THEIR CASE!!" Of more than 2,000 wild bird eggs originally collected by Bill, 517 are now stored in clear polystyrene boxes thusly labeled on their tight-fitting lids. From loons to longspurs, each egg is safely nested in Styrofoam padding, custom fit for its particular shape and size. Preserved with the eggs on faded snippets of manila paper are Bill's carefully printed observations.

HARRIS SPARROW
Artillery Lake, July 6, 1924
    Nest on ground under dwarf birch. Made of twigs, grass and moss. Lined with fine grass. 4 eggs, partly incubated. First eggs in collection.

Not only were these the first northern eggs that Bill collected, they were the first Harris sparrow eggs known to the scientific world. Before Bill ventured north, the ornithological community was largely ignorant of the nesting whereabouts of this bashful black-hooded songster.

Bill's eggs are now and forevermore stored in the Prince

of Wale's collections storeroom. This is the museum's inner sanctum of material knowledge. Treasures of ages past are stacked high on rolling metal shelves that form moving walls of immeasurable wealth. For future generations they are kept in constant darkness at a carefully prescribed humidity and temperature. The collections storeroom is accessible only through a screen of two security guards and three locked doors, two of which open electronically to a six-digit code known only to a few privileged staff.

Like the ten-thousand year-old mammoth tusk that greets you when the sanctum door swings open, like Pope John Paul II's moose antler chair adorned with walrus tusk crosses, like the wooden grave markers etched with the names of John Franklin's shipmates, the drawers holding Bill's eggs are marked with a wide ribbon of lemon yellow tape. According to the museum's official disaster plan, this tape marks "items for priority response" in the event of an emergency. Judged to be "one of a kind and irreplaceable," Bill's egg collection would be among the first treasures to go out that door to safety. Says Joanne Bird, curator of collections, "If there's a fire and we have a safe window to dash back into the museum, these are the things we would grab."

CHIPPING SPARROW
Yellowknife, June 9, 1954
    4 eggs.

Smaller than jelly beans, these eggs display a constellation of cinnamon brown spots flecked against a baby blue ground. Exquisite. Bill drilled one tiny perfect circle into the side of each egg. Undaunted by the fire of '53 that demolished his cabin and most of his eggs, Bill resumed collecting the very next spring and the next and another dozen after that. In all, he left us with over four decades' worth of springs preserved in delicate shells.

When the last of Bill's eggs were donated to the museum in 1977, they were given a monetary value of fifty thousand dollars. The man who handed them over was birdman Bob Bromley. "They're probably worth well over a hundred thousand on the black market for European egg collectors," says Bob. Measured in the currency of scientific knowledge and public education, Bill's eggs, like his many other bestowals to northern knowledge, are invaluable.

Down the hall from the collections storeroom, the museum safeguards a handful of other physical treasures from Bill's life within its catacomb like archives. Here, all that is left to us are three of his earliest field books from the 1920s, a smudged typewritten summary of mineral prospects north of a certain Lake Susu and a loose sheaf of preliminary maps on which he roughed in major rock types with grade-school pencil crayons. He portrayed the sediments in dark green, the granites in chestnut brown and the volcanics in a molten orange-yellow.

Bill's field books are slightly curved lengthwise, still conforming to the trim arc of his back pocket. The original tawny leather covers are darkly stained with sweat and grime from a field man's hands and the soot from a cabin fire that almost took his life. Within, Bill's small tidy handwriting and meticulous sketch maps are decorated here and there with the seventy-year-old corpses of inadvertently squashed mosquitoes. Everything about the field book attests that amidst the many demands of backcountry exploration—rainstorms, ill winds, a scarcity of game, a bounty of bugs—Bill was always the professional. He consistently jotted down field observations with rigorous accuracy and unreflective detachment, as one would expect from any university-trained geologist. Except for an occasional comment on the weather or the cost and weight of his handpicked provisions, the subject matter in his notes was exclusively rocks. And it was his knowledge of rocks, his pivotal role in pushing back the frontier of northern economic geology, that earned him a lasting place on a map that hitherto had been largely blank.

A colossal series of cliffs towering above the East Arm of Great Slave Lake bears Bill's surname: the McDonald Fault. So does a large body of water whose existence was flatly denied by one of Bill's early field supervisors until Bill politely led him to its shore: McDonald lake. Back in Yellowknife one of Bill's favorite haunts, where he often compared notes with fellow rock hounds became known as the McDonald Café, until it too burned to the ground like most everything else in Old Town. And to this day a lakeshore road named McDonald Drive winds through the heart and soul of a community built on gold.

"A lot of people rushed in here thinking that they'd make a fortune in a few weeks," chuckled Bill in a retrospective radio interview during his autumn years. "You know, everyone thought they could stake moose pasture, then sell it for a million dollars. Well, they soon decided that there wasn't as much gold as they first supposed. So most of them pulled out, spreading to other places. A lot of them, *very* disappointed, left the North for good."

Not Bill. For half a century he remained as much rooted to the North as the bare and pathless bedrock of the Canadian Shield. The long-shot odds of frontier prospecting and the haphazard ups and downs in the gold market did nothing to erode Bill's cardinal link to the land. This man was perennially in search of a wider wealth, unseen by many, unprofitable to most. His search was fueled by an unquenchable thirst for knowledge and charged with a quiet joyous love of all nature.

Bill's livelihood was rocks. And though he generally appreciated them with respectful equanimity—like the self-abiding Hindu mystic who "regards a clod of earth, a stone and gold alike"—Bill could get passionate about them. He ranked the discovery of the Pine Point mother lode for instance as one of the most exciting moments of his life. But Bill's grandeur vocation was mining the wisdom of the wild and for that he received no wages. No one paid him to collect those now priceless bird eggs. He alone covered both the postage and the prayers when he occasionally shipped them to eager academic colleagues in the south. No one paid him to collect all those plants, lichens, mosses, insects, fish, lampreys nor really anything other than rocks.

Bill's love for nature was unbounded. He knew the country like a fox or a weasel and traveled through it as freely by paths of his own. Whether out on a faraway prospecting mission or walking to a local coffee shop, he maintained a ceaseless curiosity and deep affection for the nuances of nature around him: the remark of a raven, the bend of a birch tree, the color of a cloud. He would leap at the chance for any excursion, treating it as an opportunity to make some new acquaintance with the land. No flower or bird or fleeting hare escaped his observing eye. His intimate attention to the subtle traits of nature was akin to that of the sage-naturalist Henry David Thoreau. A fellow Harvard classmate wrote that Thoreau's "eyes were sometimes searching, as if he had dropped, or expected to find, something. It was the look of Nature's own child learning to detect her way-side secrets. For he saw more upon the ground than anybody suspected to be there. Thus did nature reveal to him the richest treasures of her store."

The words of Ralph Waldo Emerson's eulogy to Thoreau could as easily be applied to Bill Mac.

It seemed as if the breezes brought him,
It seemed as if the sparrows taught him;
As if by secret sight he knew
Where, in far fields, the orchids grew . . .
[And] all her shows did Nature yield,
To please and win this pilgrim wise.

In September 1982, eleven years after Bill's death, the Northwest Territories' top ranking statesman, Commissioner John Parker, presided over the opening ceremonies of a new Yellowknife school, William L. McDonald Junior High. In his closing remarks Parker described Bill as "inquisitive, observant and quietly unpretentious, yet so far ahead in so many fields. He was a wonderful man and I think it's very, very fitting that he be remembered by this magnificent education structure because he was never far away from learning. He was always studying, always remembering. He had tremendously broad interests. Parker then flipped on a slide projector to present the one and only picture he could find of Bill Mac. "He practically never had his picture taken—just never thought of it, I guess. His face is shaded but at least it's something for you to look at." There was Bill, up on the screen, larger than life and, as usual, pointing to some feature on the ground.

PIKE PASSIONS

*It's a good fish, the northern pike, but probably more
than others bears the brunt of the most unfair of descrip-
tions—vicious, evil, solitary marauder, mean-looking
and rapacious, rough guy. . . . This creature cannot be
faulted for its ferocious face—that's the way Nature put
it together, and in a sense it's a masterpiece of design.*
—Frederick Wooding, Lake, River and Sea-Run
Fishes of Canada

In a recent "Lunacy Report" near the back of a Saturday
Globe and Mail, anglers learned why not to kiss a pike:

> A Russian fisherman has to go to the hospital to
> have a pike removed from his nose. The man and some
> friends are ice-fishing about 100 kilometers northwest
> of Moscow when he catches a 70-centimeter pike.
> Showing off for his buddies, he raises the fish high and
> kisses it on the mouth. The pike clamps down hard on
> the man's nose. The pike's jaws remain tightly locked
> even after the fisherman's companions behead it.
> Doctors at a hospital finally set the man free.

Just how you react to such news depends a lot on your
level of affection for pike. Its given names speak of many levels, high and low: the great northern pike, jackfish, tundra
shark, slough shark, freshwater wolf, snake, luce, slimer, the
poor man's salmon. In scientific circles this fish is known as
Esox lucius. The first part, *Esox*, was a household word for pike
throughout Europe from the Middle Ages onwards. The
species name, *lucius*, was inspired perhaps by its leering grin

reminiscent of that misguided light-bearer from hell, Lucifer.

Pike begin life innocently enough. The instant the ice begins to break up from the countless lakes and rivers of the North, adults are out there spawning. First, the sexes pair up amidst continuous gnashing of teeth between competing males. Sex hormones surge as large runs of pike storm into quiet shorelines and marshes, muscling their way through the reed-choked shallows. In fast creeks throttled by beaver dams and bedrock ledges, hundreds of bruised and restless pike gather in pools, waiting, like so many salmon, to leap and slap and thrash upstream through the white water. The sex act begins at some magic moment when the male sidles up and lingers beside the female. They do a few quick barrel rolls over each other, then swing their reproductive vents seductively close but not touching. Rapid simultaneous quivering by both fish marks the climatic release of eggs and sperm-laden milt. Each sex act ends with violent tail flicks that send the eggs aloft into the water column. This age-old dance goes on many times a day for up to five days, after which a pike nursery is well established.

A prime female pike releases thirty-two thousand amber-colored eggs during the spawning season. She builds no protective nest. All spawning pike disappear from the scene, consigning their tiny progeny to aimless drifting. But they do not drift for long. Being extremely adhesive they stick to the first thing they contact: a rock, a horsetail reed, a pond lily stem, a spruce deadhead. Millions of eggs are released in a single spawning area. Only half of them are fertile. Less than 1 percent will grow into anything resembling a pike as we know it. The rest are devoured by fish, aquatic insects, ducks, muskrats and the like. Those that beat the odds hatch two weeks later, surviving on distended yolk sacs carried aft and below their jiggling bodies. Soon they are calmly grazing on bits of algae or small invertebrates that happen to float by their puny jaws.

It is not long before the first awkward lunges begin. Into that growing mouth go red water mites, leaches, minnows and eventually their own kith and kin. Down in north Saskatchewan a fisheries biologist reported seeing a train of six fingerling pike all locked together each trying to swallow another. From the boreal woods of Manitoba comes the story of a twelve-kilogram pike that drowned trying to stuff another pike two-thirds its size into its mouth. And in Alaska there once was a fisherman who bagged two pike with one lure. It seems the hooked fish, while being reeled in, was attacked by another pike who just would not let go.

In the esteemed ichthyological handbook *Freshwater Fishes of Canada*, the pike's voracious appetite is clearly and tastefully described: "Adult pike can be classed best simply as omnivorous carnivores in that they eat virtually any living vertebrate available to them within the size range they can engulf. The optimum food size has been calculated at between one-third and one-half the size of the pike." In one year a mature pike might eat up to forty-five kilograms worth of fish, frogs, mice, ducklings, weasels and muskrats. Random stomach content analyses from the western Arctic indicate that pike also have an appetite for silver wristwatches, rubber boots (heel only), Fruit of the Loom underwear (band only) and apparently the upper plate of a pair of dentures. Pike will bite a human hand or toe dangling carelessly in the water. A determined pike once leapt clear onto a rocky shore in pursuit of my wife's red and yellow socks—while her feet were still in them.

Without doubt the pike is a mean, lean, hunting machine. The Koyukon natives of northwestern Alaska call the pike *k'oolkkoya*, "that which darts or is thrown at something." The French come more to the point and call it a *grand brochette*,

Dogrib elder prepares a pike for drying in the sun. (PHOTO: JAMIE BASTEDO)

"the big skewer." Together these names celebrate the pike's torpedo-shaped body and its ability to fling itself fast and forcefully onto its prey. In stark contrast imagine the bashful butterfly fish of the tropics with its round well-finned body specialized for making tight graceful manoeuvers in and out of the coral beds. Now imagine the portly tuna with its muscular trunk and high dorsal fins designed for prolonged cruising. The pike is a different kind of specialist, a lunge feeder, built instead for short powerful bursts of acceleration. It owes this mastery to a cylindrical body, large, back-set dorsal and anal fins plus a broad and nimble tail fin. But lunge feeders, like the pike and its saltwater cousin the barracuda, are not known for accuracy. Hence that massive mouth amply loaded with recurved teeth. These renowned assets increase a pike's chances of clamping down on prey even if its aim is a bit off.

Something in the mind or muscles of a pike makes it a survivor. It always has been. Fifty thousand years ago, when much of North America was under two kilometers of glacial ice, pike were among the few species of freshwater fish able to withstand the harsh ever-shifting weather conditions of Beringea. This ice-free land bridge stretching from the Yukon to Siberia was also home to roving bands of stalwart humans. When mammoth meat was scarce we speared and clubbed pike in the shallows. We fished for them with crude bone hooks and sewn willow nets set beneath the lake ice.

Some archeologists believe that it was in this place and time that we first domesticated wild dogs. We've been feeding them pike ever since. "Why does the puppy always start at the head of a not quite dead jackfish?" asked dog musher Fran Hurcomb, whose puppy, Pogey, inspired her to write this not-quite-a-poem. "She was part Eskimo husky and part Woodyard Special," says Fran, who lives in a houseboat on Yellowknife Bay. "I think there was some German Sheperdy stuff in there too." While collecting unemployment insurance (pogey) between jobs as a mining camp cook, Fran fell in love with a blond ball of fluff adorned with black ears and snout. "The poor little thing almost got eaten by a pike whose jaws kept snapping long after it was out of the water." The tables soon turned as Pogey took to a diet of pike, which sustained her well for the next sixteen years. During that time, Fran disfigured more than one ax blade chopping up frozen pike for her sled dogs. "Boy do they freeze hard—harder than other fish. It's like chopping a rock!" Pike are indeed tough fish. They are usually the last to expire in Fran's fish nets, often wrecking them as they go defiantly to their last reward. They fight in the nets like no other fish. They rip the meshes with their spiny teeth and twist the net around themselves as a child wrestles with a blanket while suffering nightmares.

Parked near Fran's houseboat is a fifty-meter-long covered barge. It is painted marine white from stem to stern. Above a wide metal door on its starboard side is a dull gray sign hand-painted with large black letters: Fish Plant. Each year hundreds of kilograms of fresh pike go through this door and into Nancy Buckley's freezers. "Pike isn't a quota fish, not like trout or whitefish, so we can take as many as we want," says Nancy, who works and lives inside the barge. Pike wreck Nancy's nets, too. And for bulk sales, pike fetch the lowest price: only twenty-five cents a pound, half the price of trout and a tenth that of pickerel. "It's a lot of work getting pike ready for sale— all that heading and gutting and finning." On top of this Nancy must truck her catch to Hay River, a nine-hour drive away. But the economics usually add up thanks to a growing international demand. "Pike's got a bad name," says Nancy. "The ones caught in warm southern lakes taste all muddy. But once people taste our cold-water pike, they really get hooked." Restaurateurs in France and Germany are particularly well hooked on Canadian northern pike. Delivered from the depths of Nancy's freezers, a subarctic pike might well end up on a silver platter in Paris, stuffed to the eyeballs and dressed with sweet marjoram, pickled oysters, mace, sweet claret wine, anchovies and a large sprig of fresh parsley.

Down the bay, fish bistro owner Sam Bullock helps meet the demands of local pike connoisseurs. He admits that pike are hard to fillet. "All those side bones along the lateral line can be a nuisance. I have yet to figure out the right angle to hold my knife so I can get all those little bones out. And they *are* slimy at the best of times—hard to get a good grip." But when it comes to fish chowder Sam looks in only one direction. "When you boil up a pike, it creates a nice gelatinous substance in the broth. Pike flesh holds together really well. It stays firm even after simmering for hours. Mouth-watering! For chowder I don't look at any other fish but pike. It's really good smoked too. You should try it."

Fish bistro owner Sam Bullock deftly holds a monster pike, dripping with fresh slime, before chopping it up for chowder. (PHOTO: NORTHERN NEWS SERVICE)

American anglers revere the mighty jack. From Oklahoma, Alabama, Texas and the rest, they come here to do battle. It is the number one drawing card for most back-country fishing lodges in the mainland Northwest Territories. Each summer thousands of Americans turn north off the turnpike and drive to the outer limits of the continent's road system. Somewhere just north of the Canadian border they slip into their gladiatorial gear. Camo greens and browns all over, twelve-pocketed Goretex fishing vests and baseball caps flush with tied flies. In the back of their Yankee-plated Jeeps, Land Cruisers and stretch Winnebagos are tackle boxes tiered high like church organ keyboards. Rattling inside are large spoons, plugs, bucktail spinners, worm harnesses and other hook-bearing baubles. Fuzz-e-grubs, Power Cranks and Hula Poppers. Ruby-eyed Wigglers, Krocodile Wobblers and Tasmanian Devils. They lug north whatever it takes to provoke a pike attack.

The muskellunge, puffed up cousin of the pike, streaks to the surface too soon after it's hooked. The lake trout, no matter how rotund, just plain gives up too easily. On the other hand a hooked pike wages a continuous battle, fought long and hard in the depths. Any seasoned pike hunter knows that the bend of the rod and speed of the disappearing line give no clue whatsoever as to the unseen quarry's size. A pike of any proportion will serve up a confusing mix of gentle twitches and mighty yanks—and everything in between. During the electric moments from contact to capture, one image hovers in the mind's eye of all self-respecting anglers in pike country: the biggest pike there ever was.

The official, uncontested, beyond-a-shadow-of-doubt angler record for northern pike on this continent comes from the Scanandaga Reservoir in New York State. In late September 1940 a man wearing a yellow raincoat and large grin successfully reeled in a pike that measured 133 centimeters and weighed 21 kilograms. Stoney Rapids Saskatchewan holds the all-time Canadian record with a 1954 catch at 19 kilograms. Soon after the Scanandaga incident, a respected Edmonton doctor claimed in his fastidious field notes that he pulled a 25-kilogram pike from a lake in northern Alberta.

The good doctor unfortunately took the truth of this matter to his grave, leaving no photo or stuffed mount to his heirs.

Fish this grand may reside farther north in the relatively unfished waters of the subarctic. In 1772 Samuel Hearne went out fishing on Lake Athabasca on behalf of the North West Company. His subsequent fish story is recorded with all the sincere objectivity that a great British explorer can muster: "Pike are of an incredible size in this extensive water. Here they are seldom molested, and have multitudes of smaller fish to prey upon. If I say that I have seen some of these fish that were upwards of forty pounds weight, I am sure I do not exceed the truth." It would not have been the first time Hearne beheld pike of this stature. It seems they grow much larger in Europe.

Ireland, of all places, holds the "official" world record for pike: 24 kilograms. At its belly this well-fed fish was almost a meter in girth. That was in 1920. Fish stories from northern Europe recorded three centuries earlier speak of 45-kilogram pike, some of which were big enough to pull innocent mules and milk maidens into ponds. Then there's the famous Emperor's Pike from Mannheim, Germany, caught in 1497. This fish was almost 6 meters long and weighed 250 kilograms—about the weight of a modest grizzly bear. The monster's captors, so the story goes, were amazed to find an engraved copper ring attached to its gills. On this ring were inscriptions telling of the fish's release by Emperor Frederick II in the year 1230. Accounting for the many decades it would take to grow a fish this big, they concluded that the pike was well over three hundred years old. (Twenty-five years is a ripe age for a pike these days.) Jaws dropped as common people streamed into the Mannheim Cathedral to genuflect before the miraculous skeleton. Years later the Emperor's Pike was unceremoniously removed from the cathedral and forever dismantled when it was discovered that somebody had built the skeleton by gluing together the vertebrae of several large and legitimate pike.

Few fishes, regardless of ancestry or size, enjoy as ambiguous a relation to humans as the northern pike. Master predator, chowder king, angler's dream. Net wrecker, lure thief, demonic shark of the shallows. From one end of the spectrum to the other, the northern pike wears its colors well and has earned them all. Can you say honestly that these colors remain eternally fixed in your mind, especially when suddenly confronted with a living, breathing, snapping pike more or less in your face?

"I want it, I want it!" screamed my four-year-old daughter as she hauled back on her ten-dollar blue and white plastic fishing rod. Still invisible at the other end of the line was her first pike. "I hate it, *I HATE IT!*" she screamed, many decibels louder, when her pike, a good-sized one, suddenly ripped through the glassy surface and torpedoed through the air toward our canoe. "I want it, I want it!" she cried again as the fish plunged below us, almost tugging her overboard. Equipped with the clear and spontaneous intuition of childhood, my four-year-old speaks for us all. The pike's severe countenance, arresting personality and inscrutable charm challenge our ability to judge anything in nature, big teeth or not. But whether a pike encounter inspires reverence or revulsion, there is, underlying all opinions of this creature, a shared substratum of awe.

THE ABCs OF BUG PROTECTION

Insects form the hair shirt of the north country.
−*Ted Nagle,* The Prospector North of Sixty

Biting insects give the north woods a bad name. Awaiting you there, amidst the black spruce and Labrador tea, is a distinctively Canadian torture. An evil scourge. A terrible pestilence. Flying hypodermic needles. In some cases even the scientific names ascribed to these bugs by normally impartial taxonomists reflect the prejudices born of too many bites in the bush. Among the many northern species of mosquitoes are *Aedes excrucians*, which speaks for itself, *Aedes fitchii*, which calls to mind both fidgeting and itching, and *Aedes inornata* (meaning "ugly or unseemly"), which is about as far as a taxonomist can go before labelling this species as downright repulsive.

The verdict is still out on which is worse: blackflies or mosquitoes. Prospector Ted Nagle, remembering his 1904 trip along the south shore of Great Slave Lake, cast his vote for mosquitoes.

> For sheer discomfort it is difficult to imagine anything worse than blackflies. They slipped beneath our clothing and set our skin afire. But worst of all were the mosquitoes. The number of northern mosquitoes

that appear after a hatch is unimaginably huge. We often wake up mornings to find a velvety gray ring around the campfire. Hundreds of thousands of mosquitoes had settled on the warm ground just far enough from the fire to feel safe. They rose in a cloud to fasten on anyone of us who approached them unawares.

Before squashing them Nagle sometimes took a morbid pause to closely examine their anatomy. "There were two different kinds of mosquitoes. The smaller gray ones were much like those known in the south. But there were also large yellow mosquitoes, at least half an inch long. The big yellow mosquitoes had augers on their noses that could drill through clothing."

For renowned naturalist Ernest Thompson Seton, who explored Canada's western subarctic in the early 1900s, it was blackflies, hands down, that gave him the greatest grief. "The blackflies attack us like some awful pestilence walking in darkness, crawling in and forcing themselves under our clothing, stinging and poisoning as they go."

The journals of early visitors to this region are replete with loathsome accounts of blackfly invasions. Here's another from a 1930s prospector working in the Mackenzie River Valley. After listening to the "driving rain" of flies on his tent all night, he finally braved a dash outside to make breakfast. "In a few moments, the bacon in the frying pan was mottled with hundreds of black dots—flies that had perished. In the coffeepot floated a layer that covered the whole surface."

Besides molesting humans, insect assaults on domestic animals also checker historical records from the north woods. One account from northern Alberta describes cattle keeling

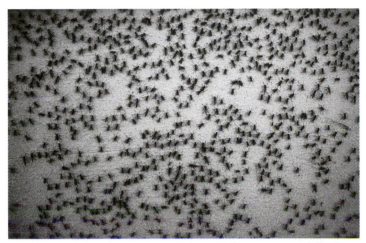

A horde of midges plasters the wall of a canvas tent. Fortunately for the occupants, these do not bite. (PHOTO: CHRIS O'BRIEN)

over dead within fifteen minutes of a blackfly attack—from some sort of mysterious shock effect, not from loss of blood. While journeying through the same region in 1915, explorer and anthropologist Vilhjálmur Stefánsson wrote of farm animals driven mad by bugs. In one journal he claimed that young calves and piglets were known to have died as a result of multiple attacks by bulldog flies and mosquitoes. In forest clearings and crude fields he observed huge smudge fires built not for farmers but for their cattle, which occasionally would slip out from the protective cover of smoke to risk a few mouthfuls of grass.

For some contemporary northerners, many of whom are recent transplants, the Bug Problem sucks all the pleasure out of their brief subarctic summers. In a desperate plea for some sort of civil defense action, one unnerved city dweller from Yellowknife shared his plight with the local newspaper editor.

As you are well aware, the mosquito population is taking over our fair town. The number of critters has reached the point where it is becoming virtually impossible to spend time outdoors without risk to ongoing blood supply. Ambulating twenty feet from one's vehicle to residence is a race for human survival. Mowing the lawn, weeding gardens, taking the dog for a walk, strolling on our well-conceived nature pathways have lost appeal due to the voracious airborne pests.

Are these simply the accounts of northern travelers and residents who have been struck blind with entomophobia, a morbid fear of insects? Or are all such horror stories true? Dr. Harold Lutz, a forestry professor from Yale University who "endured" several summer's of field work in Alaska back in the 1950s puts his faith in the stories. "The credibility of some of the accounts relating to the severity of the torture inflicted by mosquitoes is sometimes questioned," he asserts, "but only by those whose experience does not include at least one summer in the northern forests."

Come what may to the North, nothing short of another ice age will rid us of biting insects no matter how insufferable they may be. So what do we do in the meantime? Try these simple offerings: my ABCs of self-defense against bugs.

A is for Attitude. Let's face it, fighting for all-out victory against the vast northern battalions of bugs is a lost cause. Their combined biomass exceeds, by an order of magnitude, that of the million caribou that roam freely across northern Canada. Biting insects are the dominant life-form North of Sixty and in human terms always will be. Extermination is out of the question. But fighting our own bigotry against them is a battle we *can* win. The road to peaceful coexistence with our insect brothers and sisters begins with tolerance, which, said some sage, is a sapling that grows only when rooted in the soil of understanding.

Bloodthirsty? Of course they're bloodthirsty. Wouldn't you be if this was the food for which your exquisite mouth and digestive tract were so designed to process? Malicious, spiteful, purposefully needling? Such designs could not enter their little brains, such as they are. The motives of biting insects are as pure as any creature, be it grizzly or grasshopper, innocently absorbed in the act of nourishing a rapidly growing family. For instance in some species of mosquitoes the female can carry out all her life functions, even nourish her developing eggs, getting by on plant nectar alone. But blood is much richer than nectar, particularly in proteins, and can increase egg production a hundredfold. There. In the service of motherhood, are you ready to make peace?

No? Well, then consider their colossal ecological importance. Biting insects collectively pump astronomical amounts of energy into countless northern food chains. As aquatic larvae they provide food for many species of fish and ducks. Insect-eating birds such as swallows, flycatchers and warblers absolutely depend on them. For instance a lone tree swallow on the wing can gulp down as many as twenty-five hundred flying insects during a good day over the marsh. These insects also help satisfy the voracious appetites of dragonflies and damselflies, which in turn become food for many kinds of birds and the occasional frog. And in the process of foraging for nectar, they serve as the main pollinators for innumerable northern plants, including most berry bushes, a favored source of food for many animals, both four- and two-legged.

"Biting flies are a strong indicator of healthy environments," says my former biostatistics professor and bug counter, Dr. Steve Smith at the University of Waterloo. Biting flies are his entomological passion. His life would be much impoverished without them. And so would ours, he argues.

> Their absence would mean that something serious has happened to an area of wetlands and streams. Sure, we bitch all the time about mosquitoes. But the reality is, if you said "Would you live in an area without them?' I'd say no because then I wouldn't have the frogs in springtime . . . and I wouldn't have the birds associated with wetlands, and I wouldn't have the flora associated with wetlands.

Where Smith lives, in southern Ontario, wetlands exist as isolated islands surrounded by a sea of urban and rural development. In the wild and well-watered northland, moist breeding pockets for biting insects abut every hummock and hill. Here they thrive in numbers that only physicists can understand. Try to imagine, for instance, close to one hundred million squirming, wriggling mosquito larvae per hectare of breeding habitat. The ecological upshot is that such numbers represent a healthy starting quota for the multitude of organisms that absolutely depend on these bugs for survival.

The next time you are besieged by bugs keep their motives and munificence in mind. A positive attitude towards your attackers may serve as a last line of mental self-defense when all else fails.

B is for Behavior. Not theirs, ours. Exactly where and how and when you go through the north woods can make a big difference to the condition of your skin (and your nerves) upon your return to camp. One early surveyor did just about everything wrong in this respect and suffered accordingly. He described northern bugs as a plague that followed him every summer everywhere he went. This particular surveyor hap-

pened to spend most of his summers hacking rectilinear seismic lines through that jumbled patchwork of wetlands
known as muskeg. This boggy soggy landscape is dimpled
with countless small ponds and puddles. Some might call it a
waterscape. So in a sense he asked for the bugs when he took
the job. Or rather his superiors sentenced him to them when
they drew those straight lines on the map. A prisoner of pre-
determined compass bearings, he had to pass unswervingly by
terrain features that would have delivered him well out of the
reach of probing insect mouths, places shunned by bugs and
embraced by savvy northern travelers. That poor surveyor
had to walk right past places of refuge rendered bug-free
thanks to the wind.

As passive riders on the wind, mosquitoes are known to
have blown across distances approaching one hundred kilometers. But wind has a debilitating effect on both the coor-
dination and appetite of most biting insects. The stronger, the
better. Fifteen kilometers per hour seems to be the magic
threshold at which flying insects are knocked off their little
feet. So get out of the wet woods and find a high windswept
outcrop or open shoreline for your traverse or campsite.
Should the bugs persist there is no surer escape from them
than pushing off the land and paddling to a breezy platform
of water. The moral in short is to take the high trail or wind-
ward shore to reduce blood loss.

As an alternative there is always your tent if the wind has
died completely and your forbearance for bugs has evaporat-
ed. Claustrophobic in there? Instead you can simply smudge
them away by throwing a rotten punky log or a few green
spruce boughs onto the fire. Smoke is anathema to most
insects, but so is it to most campers. The trick of carefree
smudging is to place yourself close enough to the smoke to
smell it but not inhale it. Even amidst a maelstrom of mos-

quitoes, you can with practice quickly regain your composure and redirect your attention to matters of importance, like savoring your tea, watching the sun set or exchanging bear-attack stories.

In the thick of an insect infestation a smudge fire provides a practical alternative to going temporarily insane, according to geologist Charles Camsell.

> They rose up in clouds with every step I took," he wrote in 1920, while surveying the Mackenzie Valley. "I had no protection from these pests . . . and from time to time as I got tired I also became almost panicky. When I felt myself beginning to run I immediately pulled up and made a small fire so that I could get some relief in the smoke. I could easily imagine a man going off his head if he should have to endure such torture for any length of time.

Exactly *when* you choose to do your tripping—or for that matter mowing the lawn—is your business. But in bug country a proper sense of timing can help keep your blood pressure low and blood volume high. Most mosquitoes are crepuscular feeders, preferring to binge on your blood at dawn and dusk. You are safest in your sleeping bag or around the fire during these times. But get this: blackflies have an altogether different meal shift. They are generally diurnal—daytime feeders—seeking blood most intensely in the early morning and late afternoon. Should you decide to take no other precautions against bugs, this leaves you just a few hours during the hottest part of the day to hike or paddle like hell.

It's late June, peak of the bug season. You are on foot traversing a large spruce bog several kilometers from camp. You are wearing shorts, a T-shirt and a tired pair of peat-stained runners. All you have in your daypack are binoculars, a granola bar, a ball cap and last April's ski wax (it happens, I know). You are caught in the subarctic wilderness without wind, a canoe, a well-sealed tent, some matches or a watch. The whining random pulse of insect wings is rising fast. So is your dread. You can run, but you can't hide. You can, however, opt for one last surefire defense: find a lake or river or slough and jump in. They won't find you underwater.

C is for clothing. Light and tight is all you need to know. Light, since most biting insects are cued to home in on dark colors reminiscent of the tawny browns and blacks of their fur-covered natural hosts. And tight, since many biters, particularly blackflies, like to creep down collars, through loose sleeves and up dangling pant legs to find dark cosy feeding troughs (they make their own). After swallowing the last of your urban pride, button up your collar, batten down your cuffs, ram your pant legs into some thick woolen socks. Immunize yourself against attack in true northern style.

Those putting their faith in less homegrown technologies can put down a large handful of tens and buy a bug jacket. There are two main kinds. My favorite is a fine-meshed "dopeless" bug jacket equipped with elasticized ruffles from top to bottom. The ruffles serve to elevate the surface of the jacket away from your vulnerable skin. As well, they give this model the look and feel of some kind of bizarre bodice that Queen Victoria might have worn after hours. Trail chic. The other kind of jacket, *sans* ruffles, is sold with several ounces of high-proof bug repellent, which you are supposed to dump all over the jacket before putting it on. Hopefully you like the acrid smell of bug dope, because whatever clothes you slip this jacket over will be gassing off in your closet weeks after you return to civilization.

Though I am dead against them it would not be fair to omit some mention of the infamous bug hat. Perhaps I have negative associations with its use. I reserve it for emergency situations, putting it on only when the bugs are so thick I can't breathe. Furled for storage deep in your pack, the industry standard looks like a squashed bowler hat made from insipid green nylon. Unfurled, a thick sun-glinting screen drops from its rim, revealing at the bottom an elastic choking device meant for your neck. With one of these things on, you can't see straight, you can't eat or drink anything, you can't carry on intelligent conversations (even with yourself), for who could take you seriously? What is worse, when a few errant bugs manage to squirm their way past your constricting neck band, as they inevitably do, you can't for the life of you get them out. There you are, eyeball to compound eyeball with the pestiferous pip-squeaks you are trying to evade. When caught in such a pickle, I can't help thinking of the head-mounted torture device described in George Orwell's *Nineteen Eighty-Four*. Do you remember that scene? The story's hero, Winston Smith, is trapped in Room 101. "The thing that is in Room 101 is the worst thing in the world," explains his interrogator as he prepares to clamp the device over Smith's unwilling head. "It was an oblong wire cage with a handle on top for carrying it by. Fixed to the front of it was something that looked like a fencing mask . . . [Smith] could see that the cage was divided lengthwise into two compartments, and that there was some kind of creature in each. They were rats." Which is worse: a dozen caged blackflies chewing on your neck or a couple of hungry rats? I'm not sure. The bug hat. Don't leave home without one. But pray you never need to use it.

D is for dope, bug dope. My favorite: citronella oil, a natural insect repellent extracted from a sweet, lemon-scented grass of the same name that grows in southeast Asia. Though its effects are short-lived it does work, and the big cosmetic companies like Avon know it. Hence the burgeoning new line of alternative no-risk bug repellents. Alternative to what? In a word: DEET. In many words: Di-ethyl-m-toluamide. This wonder chemical was developed in the 1940s by uniformed entomologists working in secret laboratories owned and operated by the U.S. military. To a mosquito or blackfly zooming towards you on its final approach, the smell of DEET in effect jams its radar by seriously meddling with its natural impulses to land and bite. "Eureka!" said its discoverers. "A high-potency, easily fabricated, long-lasting bug repellent." Among this chemical's many wonders is what it does to your polyester pants, camera case and the varnish on your paddle. It eats them. Another wonder is that anybody of sound mind might actually apply this stuff, full-strength, to their bodies, let alone to those of their children.

It stands to reason that a chemical developed just down the hall from a laboratory developing nerve gas might make you nervous. For most users DEET causes tingling, a mild irritation and occasional desquamation (the erosion of uppermost skin layers). Apparently small sacrifices compared to the blight of bugs. But look deeper. Almost 20 percent of the DEET you apply to your skin is flowing freely through your bloodstream within one hour. And on what organ does it go to work on? Your brain of course. High concentrations of DEET (over 30 percent), when applied as directed on the spray can label, may result in varying degrees of toxic encephalopathy, a poisoned brain. According to the *American Medical Sciences Bulletin*, symptoms vary from headache, restlessness and unexplained crying spells to "rapid pressured speech, gait disturbances, and delusions of grandeur," the latter of which may explain at least some of the stories told by dope-smearing fishermen. Extreme symptoms include acute manic psychosis, writhing convulsions and "stupor progressing to coma or death." The *Bulletin* suggests that "great caution should be exercised in using DEET on children. Only the products containing the lower concentrations (usually 15 percent) should be used." Even at these levels the *Bulletin* concludes that "application should be sparing." Everything in moderation, as my father used to say. Myself, when I need a dope fix, I'll reach for sweet citronella.

Across southern Canada doping whole towns is a popular panacea to the Bug Problem. Popular at least with city councillors who would like to be seen as rectifying the apparent injustice of sharing precious urban space with a few million bugs. Starting around 1920 they used to spray waste motor oil and kerosene to coat the water surface of mosquito-infested ponds and ditches. Yuck. The idea was to suffocate the little suckers before they hatched. By the 1940s whole cities were routinely blanketed by powerful new chemical insecticides that fried the nervous systems of adult mosquitoes along with many other unintended organisms. Not environmentally kosher these days. The current rage is to spray synthetic bug hormones and so-called bacteriological insecticides all over the place and hope for best: fewer bugs and more votes. Because of the profusion of widely varying natural factors that normally dictate mosquito numbers—the rate of spring melt, amount of standing water, abundance of insect predators, direction and strength of winds, to name a few—no town in history has ever been able to conclusively say whether or not their spraying campaigns really worked. What *is* certain is that whenever proposals for spraying campaigns creep into the headlines each spring, some colorful debate soon follows.

Proponents of the new so-called environmentally friendly insecticides promise "effective relief from the insect swarms." Crusaders for a pure environment on the other hand promote personal self-sufficiency in warding off bugs while calling for an all-out ban on spraying. This debate routinely reaches a fever pitch in Winnipeg, which is ironically home of the Canada Biting Fly Institute. "The whole city is sprayed with poison by ground and air crews," wrote one longtime opponent. "Some mosquitoes and all their predators are killed; infant birth defects and allergies increase; the chemical companies show a wonderfully healthy profit; and all bodies of water soon become perfect, predator-free mosquito incubators so that even more chemical poison can be sold to the suffering and gullible taxpayers the next year."

Undaunted by such uncertain track records and possible hazards, the city of Yellowknife in the mid-1980s decided to follow suit and launch its own campaign of wholesale slaughter of mosquitoes. A familiar controversy soon buzzed its way on to the front pages of the local newspaper. "Please, I beg of you," pleaded one Yellowknife resident in favor of the plan, "Fog, spray—do *something*—to deplete the mosquito population. It has become intolerable." In the same issue, the paper's editor countered this position: "One bad bug season cannot justify the spraying of chemicals all over the place, year in and year out. We might as well ask politicians to do something about the cold temperatures during winter." The editor went on to remind his readers that no matter how effective an urban spray program may be, you can't take it with you. "Remember also that the most enjoyable part of summer in the North is not a weekend on the deserted city streets. It is out in the bush and on the water. You cannot take a publicly funded abatement program to the lake." The pro-spraying lobby won. But after a few springs of spraying yielded nothing but inconclusive results and large bills to the taxpayers (one estimate came to fifty cents per dead bug), the city decided to sell off its spraying arsenal and scrap the whole program. The wiser among city councillors now knew that spraying insecticide to kill bugs in the subarctic is like trying to subdue a volcano with a garden hose.

In India there is a small sect of Jain monks who always mask their mouths and carry with them a dainty white broom. When walking about, they use the broom to sweep the ground in front of them to avoid inadvertently crushing underfoot any of God's tiniest creatures. The mask prevents accidental swallowings of the same. In the western world, Yellowknife resident Chris O'Brien comes as near to anyone in equaling this level of respect for all life, including biting insects. During his twenties this man spent many happy hours clutching the wheel of a Formula III race car hurtling down road courses in Britain and Canada at speeds over two hundred kilometers an hour. Now a car-less naturalist in his early fifties, O'Brien has anchored himself firmly and enthusiastically to the subarctic, bugs and all.

Clear, searching eyes, silver midparted hair and a fulsome beard give O'Brien an outwardly monkish appearance. His voice is low and mellow, like that of a late night FM announcer, and he speaks with a self-effacing authority that makes you listen. When I asked him to declare whether or not he kills mosquitoes, he responded, with unfeigned sincerity, "Why should I?" He told me that under no circumstances does he willfully squish them. "There's really no point since even if you try to kill every one that lands on you, others are still going to find you and bite you. Besides, there's nothing to fear from being bit by a few mosquitoes unless you're in malaria country. I simply brush them aside. The big ones like bulldog flies—the ones that *really* hurt—I give them a good whack with the back of my hand as a kind of warn-

The bug sucker being pressed into service at one of O'Brien's wilderness camps. (PHOTO: CHRIS O'BRIEN)

ing shot. I'm telling them to bug off and look for a moose instead. It usually works." O'Brien admitted that such forms of persuasion may fail when the bugs thicken the air. In this case he dons his dopeless bug jacket then dabs a bit of 7 percent DEET cream on his neck and hands. "None of this 95 percent nonsense for me. The stuff's bloody toxic at those concentrations."

There is nothing on earth that now brings O'Brien more joy than settling into a lakeside bush camp of his choice and spending the entire subarctic spring and summer observing in Thoreau-like fashion the ever-changing face of nature. Standard equipment amidst his humble camping gear is what he calls a bug sucker. It consists of a rigid tube with a clear wide-bore compartment attached to one end. Most people use this device to siphon up gunk from the bottom of their home aquarium. O'Brien uses it to live-trap mosquitoes. "The fellow at the pet store helped me put it together. The

Live-captured mosquitoes await release from O'Brien's bug sucker.
(PHOTO: CHRIS O'BRIEN)

only modification is some fine netting at the tube end so I don't inhale the bugs." Before retiring for the night, he applies his bug sucker to the canvas walls of his tent, gently sucking any deviant mosquitoes and blackflies into the screened holding compartment, then releasing them *en masse* back into the wilds where they belong.

O'Brien's benign equanimity towards bloodlusting insects is the product of disciplined patience, logistical preparedness and a heartfelt belief that everything in nature has its place. "They belong here as much as you do," he told me bluntly. "There are simple ways of getting around them." O'Brien bucks more orthodox views that would welcome mass extinctions of northern bugs. He does this by demonstrating quietly but convincingly that a state of peaceful coexistence with them is not only desirable but attainable. Before we get there, those of us with harder hearts or more stubborn prejudices can take solace in the words of a Yellowknife woman who was stopped on the street one buggy June day by a local newspaper reporter and asked, "What do you think of the mosquitoes?" In her thoughtful reply she likened them to "the five o'clock rush hour and warm beer"—things we ultimately can learn to live with given the right frame of mind.

LIFE AT THE EDGE

Despite being rated "the most beautiful flower of Britain," the buckbean is often unrecognized by north-western foragers.
—*Janice Schofield,* Discovering Wild Plants

I should have had a big skin drum propped between my legs and a couple of heavy bone mallets to bang it with. *Boom, boom.* Stroke, stroke. At that moment, with the mellow evening sun on my face and a playful breeze off the lake, I would have settled for a set of bongos. *Bonk, bonk.* Stroke, stroke. The sound of many paddles slicing the water more or less in unison appealed to my feral side. It called me to forsake all responsibilities and reason in exchange for an unscheduled canoe trip across Canada. Drumless, I felt I should at least clap in time to the primal beat of wood on water. Instead I kept a firm grip on my trusty Bushmaster binoculars while trying to balance two field guides on my lap. The bird guide was open to a well-thumbed page showing ducks in flight. A female bufflehead had just flown low across our bow, and I knew I would get some questions. The plant guide lay closed for the moment.

Propped tentatively against the bow thwart right in front of me was a frail but friendly woman in her early seventies. She wore a floppy straw sun hat well suited to the flower-choked promenades and sheltered urban parks of her native Victoria. Fresh gusts now toyed with her hat, obliging her to tug it down between just about every paddle stroke. While cautiously boarding the canoe this woman had told me that ever since she was a child she had always dreamed of "doing the North." This was her first trip North of Sixty. "And likely my last," she was quick to add with a shy fleeting smile that revealed hints of a girlish grin. I took that as a polite prod for me to cram as much of the outdoors into the next two hours as possible. A quick take on her crisp unfaded jeans, chalkwhite tennis shoes and pallid skin suggested to me that where she may have lacked in bush experience, she made up for in earnest enthusiasm. Though tourists' names often drift right through my brain unlogged, I made a point of silently reciting hers: Emily.

Emily suddenly stopped paddling altogether and grabbed both gunwales. "What the heck was *that?*" she asked while peering ahead past my right shoulder.

I showed her the bird guide, pointing to a demure little brown and white duck with a sliver of white on her cheek. "Is this what you saw?"

"It was just a brown blur," she said.

"That's what *I* just saw," I said. "A female bufflehead, the North's smallest diving duck."

We talked about divers and dabblers for a while until a low-flying bald eagle soared directly over us, stilling all tongues, including mine. It wheeled silently toward the pink granite shore, then effortlessly alighted on top of a jack pine not a hundred meters away. Everyone spontaneously stopped paddling as we drifted past the eagle and into a shallow sheltered bay at the south end of the lake.

Sitting backward in the bow, I faced twelve inquisitive people, none of whom I knew except for the sternman. I had met him the day before and at least knew his name, an easy one to remember: Lee Smith. Lee owned the eight-meter-

long Voyageur canoe in which we traveled. His face was lean
with an angular jaw. His thick tapered mustache swept up
slightly at each end. He had one red bandanna drawn snugly
over his head and another wrapped and knotted around his
swarthy neck. A wide Métis sash was wrapped like a cum-
merbund around his waist and knotted jauntily over one hip.
Its handwoven colors—red, yellow and a touch of blue—
echoed those of the North West Company. I would like to
believe that Lee had a hand-carved pipe or a box of snuff
tucked in one of the pockets of his rawhide vest. Back at the
beach I watched him slip comfortably into the stern, and I
knew then and there that this was as close as I would ever get
to sharing a canoe with a genuine *courier de bois*. Little did I
care that Lee wore a shirt and tie during his government day
job. Little did I care that after this evening's paddle, I probably would never see most of my shipmates again as long as I
lived. One man told me that twenty-four hours after our
tour, he would be back in his penthouse apartment over-
looking San Francisco Bay.

Such is the nature of eco-tourism in my neck of the
woods, maybe everywhere. Strangers come together in the
outdoors to explore as intimately as possible a briefly shared
piece of the planet. Then they disperse in random directions,
though most often southward, hopefully enriched, most often
forgotten. Some want to know all there is to know about the
rocks. Some are focused exclusively on birds. Others have a
fixation for flowers. Still others can't wait to see a black bear
or white wolf. A few are content simply to "learn their
berries" and eat them on the spot. I have yet to meet anyone
who openly admits having a special affection for aquatic
plants, floral species that grow under, on or up through the
water.

The bald eagle was now well behind us. People started

Yellow pond lily pads form suspended stepping stones for a wood frog. A cattail marsh rims the shore in background. (PHOTO: JAMIE BASTEDO)

working their paddles again, trying to get back in the groove of synchronous motion and reduce collisions among wayward paddles. I, the boatswain and tour guide, cheerily yelled my "stroke, stroke" routine to help smooth things out until Lee yelled back, "WHOA." Everyone stopped paddling. I twisted around to see what was coming next. We were near-

ing a dense cattail marsh at the end of the bay. I had warned
Lee that it could get shallow in there. We could get stuck. But
I felt compelled to press on since my first quarry lay along
the margin of cattails. I leaned carefully over the bow and
looked down into limpid emerald water. We were just barely
clearing the tea-colored marsh muck below. "Left, Lee," I
yelled, shooting my left arm over the gunwale. A canoe this
size does not give up its momentum easily, and Lee deftly
steered us into deeper water without a stroke. A few seconds
later, "Right, Lee," and out went my other arm. Then, "STOP,
LEE!" Plowing silently into the muck, we skidded to a stop a
few meters away from a fencelike stand of cattails.

Half-submerged at the base of the cattails was the specimen I was looking for. "There it is!" I cried as I slipped off
my gum boots and socks. I had spotted it the previous afternoon during my reconnaissance tour by kayak. I had paddled
here alone and in spite of a drenching rain was genuinely
thrilled to find a fully intact free-floating rhizome of a yellow
pond lily. It is virtually impossible to pry these things from
the bottom with a stick or paddle. To catch them in their
prime, you must risk hypothermia by diving for them in the
early spring.

"What the heck is *that?*" said the ever-inquisitive Emily.

"I'll show you," I said. It was my turn to grab both gunwales.

"You're not going in *there* are you?" asked a nonplussed
man behind her. In his Bermuda shorts and Hawaii shirt this
bearded portly fellow struck me as either a banker or a baker.
His profession, however, like everyone else's on board, was
irrelevant to the subject at hand. Such is nature's levelling
power. I looked the man squarely in the eye and offered him
my hand.

"Care to join me? It's really the *only* way to learn your

aquatic plants." He let go a nervous snicker, then heartily declined.

I rolled up my thin cotton medical pants (they dry fast), then sprang boyishly out of the canoe. It was like wading through cold molasses.

"Ugh," said somebody.

"Better you than me," said another.

I somehow made it to the cattails and victoriously lifted the rhizome high out of the water. It had the general shape and size of a modest loaf of French bread. Its surface was light brown, covered in spirals of knobby ridges and dark recessed blotches.

"Any guesses?" I asked.

"Some kind of root?" somebody said.

"Close," I said. "It's actually part of a stem, a swollen underground stem from a yellow pond lily. It's called a rhizome and is absolutely packed with starch energy. Beavers and muskrats love them. For moose it's like a giant Milkbone."

I stretched out my arms to permit closer inspection of the rhizome by my ambivalent audience.

"Cool!" said a ten-year-old boy wearing a Blue Jays ball cap and mirrored sunglasses. "It looks like a sawed-off dinosaur tail."

A pig-tailed eight-year-old two seats ahead of him told me, "It stinks." Her mother smiled at me apologetically.

True, a musky rankness hovered in the calm evening air, a boreal bouquet unlocked from the freshly exhumed peat now oozing between the toes of my size twelve feet. Those unversed in wetland ecology call it loon shit. In my mind it has a wholesome sweet smell. I take to the aroma of northern wetlands the way a prairie farmer imbibes the smell of freshly spread cattle manure. Let such odors permeate your clothes, your work and your subconscious for days on end and they inevitably become a part of you. Familiar, non-threatening, welcomed in fact.

I brought my prized specimen close to my nose and sniffed hard. The kid was right. It did stink. The aroma of freshly disturbed peat took second place to the pungent fetor of death and decay. As my face involuntarily crinkled, the girl with a better nose than I said, "Gross!" Playing upon this theme a bit, I cracked the rhizome over my knee to show my increasingly restless passengers its gooey dark brown insides. Rotten to the core. It reminded me of the mucilaginous Marmite one of my grad schoolhouse mates used to spread on his morning toast.

"We're too late to cook up this thing," I announced. I then explained that had we arrived earlier, we, like the Cree and Chipewyans before us, could have roasted, boiled, fried or dried this rhizome for food. We could have sliced up the inner center and added it like water chestnuts to a shore-lunch soup or casserole. Or we could have pulped it up with butter and seasonings like mashed potatoes.

The restlessness subsided. Our canoe was listing to port. I noticed that most people were now leaning toward the specimen, captivated by this speckled storehouse of energy, habituated to its stink. The grossed-out girl had her arm over the side, probing the marsh muck for more pond lily rhizomes. Instead she pulled up a coontail. Draped limply across her palm was a delicate underwater plant displaying layered whorls of lacy green leaves. It looked like the tail of a water-logged raccoon.

"What the heck is *that?*" I asked her, politely feigning ignorance.

She shrugged, then said, "Seaweed, I guess." To those new to pond ecology all aquatic plants are seaweed, all gulls are seagulls. Seaweed belongs in the ocean. Gulls deserve to be known by their proper names. While I told her the raccoon story she reached in for more. This time she hauled out a handful of the stuff and began scrutinizing it a few centimeters from her sensitive nose. I was glad there were at least a couple kids on board. Their reservoirs of wonder were still deep. Hers was spilling out to other passengers.

"What are those little brown things?" asked the man in front of her.

"Snails," I said. "Hundreds of baby snails." I explained how the coontail's frilly foliage shelters or feeds many kinds of aquatic life: snails, aquatic insects, frog eggs, fish fry. Life is relatively safe and easy among the coontails—until a passing duck or muskrat eats you while chowing down a mouthful of this delectable plant.

I pulled my bare feet from the squishy depths and folded myself back into the bow of the canoe. "Onward, Lee," I cried.

"Wait!" shouted a man somewhere near the stern. "What's that little yellow one over there," he asked, pointing with his paddle, "just behind that log?"

Emily leaned quickly to one side in a manner that would surely have dumped any canoe smaller than ours. She seemed to be loosening up and now leaned half overboard, looking for something small and yellow. I couldn't see anything from my position, and we were still stuck in the muck, so I swung my legs over the side once again and slithered back in. As the loonshit again took hold of my legs, it occurred to me that someone might like to join me on this excursion. Without a word I looked back at Emily and wiggled my eyebrows.

"I'm not quite up to it," she said though her body language said otherwise. I turned to the youngsters, thinking of the words of Tom Brown Jr., one of America's most acclaimed outdoorsmen: "If you are going to the beach, the woods, the swamps, or the wilderness," writes Brown in his *Field Guide to Nature and Survival for Children*, "really get into it, roll in it, and get rid of all the protection that will separate you from fully appreciating where you are. Become alive, not removed and insulated, and teach your children to do the same." I figured it was time for an educational roll in the muck.

"What about it?" I asked the mirror-eyed boy.

"Not a chance!" he said. "You think I'm crazy?" The young girl was game, but her beseeching glance into her mother's eyes was met with a silent smile and shake of the head. And so I slogged alone over to the log in question. Sure enough, right behind it was a tidy little plot of yellow bladderworts sticking their big long-lipped flowers out of the water. I stopped suddenly, then thrust my palm policeman-style back at the canoe.

"Beware!" I said, not taking my eyes off the bladderworts. "These are meat-eating flowers."

"*Those* little things?" asked the man who spotted them.

"Wait there," I said. With conspicuous caution I reached down into the muck and plucked out a specimen—"In the name of public education," I assured everyone—then slogged back to the side of the canoe. "Actually you have nothing to fear unless you're no bigger than a water flea," I said. I held the specimen up for all to see. It was smaller than the coontail, with kinkier leaves, suggesting an overworked bottle brush. Dangling on a long naked stalk was a lone yellow flower that seemed hugely out of proportion to the rest of the plant.

"Is that the eating end?" someone asked.

"No, here it is," I said, drawing a separate branch away from the main stem. Tiny translucent sacs were strung like Christmas lights along the branch. "Behold the bladders of

The yellow pond lily—a wealth of food resources and beauty.
(PHOTO: JAMIE BASTEDO)

the flat-leaved bladderwort," I said. "These things have been described as the most sophisticated trapping devices found among carnivorous plants." I described how the elastic-walled bladders have a hair trigger near their "mouths." When a hapless protozoa or other aquatic invertebrate brushes against this trigger, a flipper of tissue springs open and water rushes into the bladder, literally gulping the prey in with it. The mouth then clamps shut behind it. Large prey such as mosquito larvae are eaten in stages, head first.

"Cool!" said the mirror-eyed boy.

Afloat once again, we steered a course that took us near the south shore of the bay. The water was deeper there, and I knew there were some floating gardens along the way. "A little more right, Lee," I said. I trained my eyes on the bottom of the lake. The shadow of our moving canoe knifed through round clusters of large reddish leaves: the basal rosettes of yellow pond lilies. Reaching up to the light from the center of each rosette was a fat stalk topped with a large round bud. As we moved into shallower water, we entered a broken carpet of lime-green lily pads. "Back-paddle," I called, "and take it easy on the lily pads." Those who knew how to back-paddle, back-paddled. By the time we stopped, we were among the lily flowers.

"How could such a nice flower have such an ugly root?" asked the man from San Francisco.

"It wasn't a root. It was a *rhizome*," said my new pig-tailed assistant.

I reached into the water and plucked one of the shining flowers, just one. The cameras came out. "Pretty isn't it," I said drawing it up into the sunlight. Click, click. The orange-yellow flower cup was a little smaller than a tennis ball. The large barrel-shaped pistil in the center was still light green. "Ever try pond lily popcorn?" I asked everyone, almost rhetorically. No one had. "When this fruity part in the center goes dark green or red, you can pry out the little brown seeds and fry them up just like popcorn. They don't jump around in the pot as much as real popcorn, but they taste great." Silence. Several raised eyebrows. I think they thought I was kidding. I must do a demonstration sometime. Then I added, "Some people boil up the seeds like oatmeal and have it for breakfast."

"Do *you?*" somebody asked.

"Not regularly," I said, hating to disappoint them. "Did you know this is one of the most innocent flowers you're ever likely to meet?" I asked, still holding the pond lily and pulling a field notebook out of my pack. I opened it to a quote by an herbalist of old who had a special fondness for water lilies. From my bow seat pulpit I read, "This plant has often been used as a symbol of purity and chastity, for the water lily flower holds itself erect as if disdaining to touch the

Filigree flowers of the buckbean. (PHOTO: JAMIE BASTEDO)

murky water surrounding it." This herbalist went on to say how the family name for water lilies, *Nymphaeaceae*, translates roughly into "water virgin." He maintained that water lilies were once believed to subdue sexual aspirations and were used in various art forms to represent virginity. The name of the herbalist who reported this tidbit was Lust.

There was more to this floating garden. Even as the pond lilies receded behind us, some smartweed was tickling our bow. It was a small patch, as they often are, and we skimmed right through it before I could give the back-paddle command. Luckily I had time enough to pluck one off the surface. The flower head was a pillar of pink just a bit wider and longer than a cigarette butt. It was surrounded by supple spear-shaped leaves. I held my catch high, then sent it around the canoe for close inspection.

"Let me introduce *Polygonum amphibium*, the water smartweed," I said.

"What's so smart about it?" asked the mirror-eyed boy.

I had heard that one before. Kids think alike. "It's not their brains. It's what their leaves do to our skin. They once were used medicinally to treat ailments of the human hindquarters," I said, patting the back of my soaking pants. "Trouble is, they have quite a sting, so they used to call it 'ars-smart.'"

The parade of showy plants continued, knocking flat the widely held notion that the subarctic is botanically barren. Coming up dead ahead was a flotilla of moonflower, marsh clover, water shamrock, bitterworm or bog hop—all one and the same species otherwise known as *Menyanthes trifoliata*. I call it buckbean. Lee parked us among the flowers without me saying a word. We exchanged friendly nods over the side of the canoe. It seemed to me that he too was getting hooked on these plants. All around us were clusters of snow-white flowers that rose high above the water. They were surrounded by triads of sturdy egg-shaped leaves reminiscent of clover. The flowers were in their finest. Each of their five delicate petals was fringed with an untamed thatch of fine crooked hairs.

"What kind of name is that—buckbean?" asked a recent convert who had not said a word till now. "It doesn't look like a bean," she said.

We talked about the bean part: its leaves resemble those of

bean plants grown in European gardens. And the buck part: some think that came from *sharbock*, German for "scurvy." Rich in Vitamin C, buckbean leaves were once brewed as a cure for this killer disease. We discussed how this plant is a kind of floating medicine chest. The rootstocks, they say, are good for relieving constipation, gas pains and rheumatism. The botanical name, *Menyanthese*, means "month flower," referring to its use as a cure for menstrual pain. The home beer makers on board—there were three—perked up their ears when I told them about the traditional use of this species' leaves as a substitute for hops. Hence *bog hop*, a name that could grow on me.

We lingered among the buckbeans long after the questions waned. Someone thought they had seen a huge pike down there, and now everyone was squinting down into the water, determined to see it next. I lightly stroked a buckbean flower with the tip of my baby finger. Stunning. So perfect. So ephemeral. In a week this miracle would be shriveled and brown. My desire to move on faltered. This flower gave my spirit a firm grip on summer, and I did not want to let go. A California gull landed on the water near us, presuming maybe that we would catch and clean that pike and leave the guts behind.

"Do you get many seagulls up here?" asked my San Francisco friend, ending my brief reverie on summer's passage.

"None, actually," I said, and with that all the talk turned to birds.

We broke away from the sheltered bay and paddled headlong into a playful late evening breeze. Stroke, stroke, stroke. Like the wind, the waves on the open lake seemed indecisive. Laughter greeted the odd wave that tipped its crown into our advancing canoe. Emily's straw hat finally surrendered to the clutch of the wind, then the waves. Too late to turn around and fetch it. I made a few apologetic noises to Emily.

"Don't feel bad," she said. Her girlish grin was wider now and warmer. "It was worth it."

Though our company of strangers had left the beach less than two hours before, there was a genuine *esprit de corps* ripening among us. Every two seconds the low-angled sun ignited twelve wet paddles in a simultaneous flash of golden-orange light.

A red-throated loon let loose its barking laugh some-where over our heads. Still facing the stern I automatically raised my arm, and all paddles stopped flashing. It laughed again. Though none of us saw it, most people heard it. "It's a great place to live," I said, "where you share the lakes with four species of loon." I ran through them all: the red-throated, the yellow-billed, the Pacific and, that icon of so many Canadian coffee cups and sweatshirts, the common. "I once got bit by a common loon while skinny dipping. I saw it coming right at me underwater. . . ."

My loon story, a true one, was interrupted by something long and green on the water right beside me. "Well, lookee here," I declared. "Richardson's pondweed way out here. It must have been uprooted in a storm." I couldn't resist this opportunity. I hauled all two meters of the plant on board and wrapped its translucent wavy leaves around my arm. We drifted out there in the middle of the lake while I spoke of my favorite underwater plant, of the kelplike pondweed forests near my cabin that I joyfully skin dive through each summer, of this species' extraordinary importance to marsh animals and birds, of its celebrated oxygen output that keeps many fish alive when locked for months under a meter of ice, of the travels and tribulations of John Richardson, the sur-geon naturalist who joined Sir John Franklin on his arctic quest and after whom this species is named. All this exuberance and a stiff broadside wind had put us way off course. But since all but Lee and I were on holidays, no one seemed to care. "Steer a course for home, Lee," I cried in my best Ahab voice.

Less than two hundred strokes from the beach, my eyes riveted on a small cattail marsh along a piece of shoreline I had neglected to scout the day before. Here was another fine plant specimen that called for our attention. Should I or shouldn't I respond this close to home base?

"Hard left rudder, Lee," I cried, and before anyone had time to debate this manoeuver, I was over the side. The water was deeper than I had expected. This was more of a swim than a wade. But at least there was no loon shit underfoot. Wasting no time I lunged toward the shore without a word of explanation to my crew. There, nestled coyly among the cattails, was the object of my desire: a stately clump of water arums.

Large heart-shaped leaves formed a deep green wreath around a scattered array of one-sided lily white flowers— bantam versions of the giant skunk cabbage bloom. Loath to pick one of these relatively rare beauties, I splashed back to the canoe and grabbed the bow rope. Without deliberation I told my captives, "You've gotta see this one." Most were still in the mood. The kids seemed distracted by a young campfire crowd on the beach, but I did my best. "Meet the water arum, *Calla palustris*, which literally means 'the beautiful marsh plant.' Its beauty is matched only by its toxicity."

I told them about the overly curious botanist from Alaska who insisted on tasting this plant in spite of knowing about its peppery and poisonous acids. "In my boiled calla taste test," she wrote, "the initial pleasant flavor was quickly replaced by intense throat-on-fire sensations." Someone

Water arum, as poisonous as it is beautiful. (PHOTO: JAMIE BASTEDO)

breathing fire after a similar test gave this species another name: water dragon.

I was about to hop back into the canoe when Emily exclaimed, "Wait a minute! You haven't told us anything about those cattails."

I slapped my forehead with my wet palm. "Of course! Forgive me. The supermarket of the swamp." Now, at the end of our tour, I was wondering where to begin—the cattail has so many uses. I started with food. "Do you want to start from the top down or bottom up?" I asked. We reached a quick consensus: top down. I returned to the shore and took hold of a green hot dog affair on top of the tallest cattail. "Perfect for cattail corn on the cob." In early summer the immature female flower can be boiled and buttered as a bush substitute for sweet corn. I kneeled in the water and ran my thumb and forefinger down the stem. The tender inner core of the spring stems ranks high on the bush connoisseur's list of fine foods. "It's cheaper than asparagus and at least as tasty," I said. Then, after a few moments of underwater probing, I up-ended the plant and proudly displayed its rhizome. *"Much* easier to harvest than those pond lily things," I said. It looked like a turnip stretched sideways and covered in thick wiry roots. The Chipewyan name for cattail is *tlh'oghk'a*, "grass-fat," referring to the nutritious rhizome, which they say "is just like fat inside." I told my floating listeners how one botanist predicted that the cattail rhizome "could well become one of the wonder foods of the twenty-first century." It's around 40 per cent starch and has the same protein content as rice. A nutritious and pleasant-tasting flour can be made out of it—over one and a half metric tons per hectare of cattails. I let that sink in for a moment, then said, "Just imagine, cattail farms lining these shores a hundred years from now."

The sun was about to set. The mosquitoes were about to attack. I decided not to push my luck. I shoved the canoe offshore and hopped in for the last time. But my accolades for the cattail continued even as we paddled into the homestretch. Your flashlight gives out on you while out camping? Soak a mature cattail spike in cooking oil or kerosene, and it will burn brightly for half an hour. Your neck is stiff from too many pillowless nights in a tent? Stuff the fluffy down of cattails into your T-shirt and *voila*, instant bush pillow (cattail down is still widely used to fill kids' stuffed toys). Need some extra insulation for you boots or mitts? Cram them with the same. Run out of diapers out there or need some emergency medical dressing? Use guess what. Forget your toothbrush again? Use the fuzzy stem, where all that down used to be. And what about the cattail's long papery leaves? Baskets, bedding and high-backed chairs. Thatch for your lean-to and caulking for your cabin. And the dry rigid stem? Make an arrow for your bow.

"This plant of many gifts lets you one-stop shop in the

bush," I said in closing. I might have raved on, but Lee interjected, more interested at the moment in saving the bow of his precious canoe from destruction.

"Back-paddle!" he yelled, and this time everyone put on the brakes.

We chatted on the beach till after the sun went down. Several stragglers wanted to hear the rest of my loon story. The mirror-eyed boy wanted to know where he could get more of those "creepy pond lily roots" to scare his friends. The pig-tailed girl wanted to know if she put bladderwort plants in her aquarium, would they eat her guppies. Emily wondered whether she could find any of the plants we'd seen tonight back in Victoria. If she didn't come north again, she hoped to at least visit with some of the acquaintances she had made up here. I encouraged her to join a local naturalist group. "They could tell you what grows where," I said. Lee eventually broke up the party by recruiting us all to help him get that mother of all canoes out of the water.

Someone at park headquarters had billed that tour as a geology-*cum*-birding bonanza. We did look at some pretty rocks. We did see a few ducks and that eagle (no seagulls). But mostly we looked at water plants, an unusual eco-tour to say the least. Imagine if we had billed the tour originally for that subject alone. "Come one, come all to explore the wonderful plants of the water's edge!" Who would show up? Probably no one. Certainly not enough to do justice to Lee's big canoe.

Why the lack of interest? Largely unrecognized and unloved by the Canadian public, these water plants serve as lungs for our lakes and rivers, stabilizers for our shores, anchors for minuscule life-forms that support far-reaching food chains, nurseries for fish and frogs, filters for polluted water and of course food for countless water birds and mammals—not the least of which is us. And many species are as pretty as they are practical. Yet the only people I know who are familiar with more than two or three aquatic plant species are duck biologists.

Is it because these plants grow in places too wet, too inaccessible or too buggy for most people to discover them? Perhaps, although think of the Canadian hordes that paddle or sail or swim right past them every summer. Another factor is the dearth of publicly palatable literature on the subject. One popular field guide to edible plants of the subarctic features sixty species considered to be the most appetizing. Only one of them is truly aquatic: the yellow pond lily. What's worse is that unlike Australia, Holland, Japan, China, even New Guinea, to name a few places, Canada as a whole has no field guide dedicated to the identification and enjoyment of its aquatic plants. Such guides exist for just about each of the fifty American states, New Jersey included. Here we are right next door, one of the most well-watered countries on earth with next to nothing to entice potential aquatic plant buffs out of the closet.

Each year thousands of Canadians go to their graves having gone through life blind to the beauty of the bladderwort or water arum, uninitiated to the taste of fried cattail stems or popped pond lily seeds and oblivious to the texture of buckbean flowers and coontail leaves. Perhaps we can learn something from Asia, where the venerated lotus—distant cousin of our water lily—was chosen as the symbolic throne and footstool for their pantheon of deities. Rooted in the depths, rising to the light, swaying with the currents and nurturing the life around it, the lotus embodies the collective beauty and bounty bestowed upon us by aquatic plants. They may live at the murky edge of awareness, but they deserve a place at the clear center of our hearts.

A case in point: Emily. About the time Lee was stowing his Voyageur canoe for the winter, she wrote me a letter in appreciation for that night on the water. Apparently she found much lasting nourishment while floating amidst the buckbeans and the lilies.

I'm home and alive and haven't seen a mosquito in weeks. On the downside of course there are more people in Victoria than all of the Northwest Territories and it seems like it hasn't stopped raining since I got back.

I wanted to thank you for your tour. It's always wonderful to have a resident expert along to point out the miracles of nature. I enjoyed our paddle tremendously (even though I lost my hat!). I may yet return in a few years to explore more of the sights. In the meantime I have joined the Victoria Natural History Society and am making some very interesting discoveries in my own backyard. I also invested in a sturdy pair of gum boots to help me explore the water's edge. Until your tour, I'd forgotten that this was a favorite pastime of my youth!

Yours,
Emily

FOOTPRINT OF FIRE

From a very extensive personal knowledge of the conditions of the forests of Northern Canada, I am able to state that fires have become more and more frequent as we approach the present time.
—*Robert Bell,* Forest Fires in Northern Canada, 1888

WIELDING FIRE

Fire from the sky. It's an old story. Soon after plants first rose out of the sea to colonize the land a little over 400 million years ago, lightning-sparked fires were striking them down. From then on the geological record is riddled with fossil evidence of forest fires. The record shows that from Newfoundland to Alaska, the perennial rise and fall of northern forests has always marched in time to the drumbeat set by fire. The warp and weft in the boreal tapestry is, and perhaps always will be, dictated by fire.

How could it not be? This kingdom of highly resinous spruce and pine trees is notoriously flammable. Exposed to the right mix of low humidity and high temperatures, these trees will more or less explode. Up north, where the conifers reign supreme, forest fires can be monstrously destructive. Yet, as explained by a Dene trapper, "Whoever created the world, created lightning. If lightning starts fires, he's doing it for a reason." The same forests sacrificed to the flames in fact *depend* on fire for their long-term health and vitality. Like the mythical Phoenix bird that rises anew from its funeral pyre, a new forest, in time, rises from the ashes of destruction, its soil enriched, its vigor restored and its floral and faunal diversity greatly enhanced. This too is an old story into which we humans have woven some colorful threads.

Among the storytellers are a handful of fire historians whose specialty is to inquire into the nature and frequency of northern forest fires through time. Though few in number, they declare unanimously that this fiery wheel of destruction and renewal started rolling steadily through boreal forest soon after trees first established themselves at the end of the last ice age. By what means could they gaze into those flames extinguished so long ago? They meditated upon the signature of fossil pollen grains and plant spores preserved in cores of ancient sediments. They dug down into soils, looking for fragments of charcoal and ash. They examined the shifting patterns of annual tree rings across the North. They also plowed through old forest inventories, archival photographs, field journals and dusty government reports in search of clues to the North's fire history. And they found them.

Fire historians have dated the oldest northern fires with remarkable accuracy using sediment cores pulled from the bottom of subarctic lakes and bogs. These cores show for instance that fires were burning in the Great Bear Lake region at least seventy-six hundred years ago. Sediment cores from farther west reveal that parts of the Yukon were on fire as far back as nine thousand years ago. This makes sense given that the Yukon was much less heavily glaciated, if not totally ice-free, allowing forests to establish themselves much earlier.

But what puzzles fire historians is the discovery of a striking trend in the northern fire record. Within the last two thousand years the frequency of forest fires in the northwest has escalated dramatically. This raises some interesting questions. Was this increase in fires triggered by a corresponding climate change that brought longer, drier or stormier summers? Or does this trend bear witness to a new kind of flame spreading across the North, a flame sparked by human hands? No one knows.

Fire historian Stephen Janzen is confident that a combination of good science and more field studies may some day solve this puzzle. In the meantime he remains convinced that "No matter how limited the effect, fire in the hands of man surely altered the pattern of forest fires." In his meticulously researched history of fire in the Northwest Territories, austerely entitled *The Burning North,* Janzen discloses a special fascination with that magic moment when people first made use of fire in the North. When, he asks, did "fire in the pristine forest become fire the cultural event?"

On that unknown day when humans first set foot in the subarctic, fire became the cultural bottom line. During the frigid northern winters, only fire could create a safe microclimate for humans holed up in their skin tents. In short, no fire, no people. Therein lay at least one potential source of forest ignition besides lightning: runaway campfires. But the accounts of early explorers, missionaries, fur traders, prospectors and surveyors are rife with stories describing how native people intentionally torched the forest on a regular basis. As a survival tool fire did more than heat their tents and cook their food. They used it profitably to alter their world. Applied at the right time, in the right place, fire gave them more food, more fuel, better overland travel, improved communication and with luck fewer bugs. "In the hands of northern man," writes Janzen, "fire's utility was truly astounding."

Native people assumed the role of fire managers soon after they took up residence in the boreal forest thousands of years ago. This is at least what anthropologist Henry Lewis deduced after comparing traditional burning practices, or pyrotechnologies, from one end of the earth to the other. Cree and Athapaskan stories about ancestral uses of fire in northern Canada show remarkable parallels to those told by Australian aborigines. Elders from both groups, so culturally and ecologically distant, stressed the value of fire for improving habitats used by favored game species. Whether it was kangaroo or moose on their respective menus, these bush dwellers knew that a well-timed touch of fire to the meadows and riverbanks could have a multiplying effect on local wildlife.

Lewis took his passion for pyrotechnologies to northwestern Alberta, where he made some interesting discoveries. By interviewing local elders he learned that once the exploitive fur trade mentality sank in and trapping became a way of life, natives shifted their burning targets to include habitats used by animals wearing the most prized pelts, namely beaver, fox and marten. As it was told to Lewis, these fires were usually well controlled with natives using fire management techniques they had perfected over the millennia. The chosen habitat—be it a cattail marsh, a jack pine forest or streamside willows—was torched in the spring when the snow, a natural fire retardant, still lay on the ground. Besides giving a boost to wildlife, northern natives also used fire to increase local supplies of firewood itself. They knew that nothing prepares a spruce tree for the hearth better than a good forest fire. If it is hot and high enough, it leaves trees stripped of both bark and branches: easy to cut, easy to haul, clean to burn.

Another postfire bonus well known to early natives was its purging effect on the forest's typically tangled undergrowth, which sometimes made overland travel impossible. These boreal nomads did not think twice about setting fire to a dense forest to improve access to important hunting or fishing areas. While on the move hunting parties often communicated their whereabouts to one another by torching the moss or an isolated spruce tree. These signal fires sent up a distinctive shaft of "fresh dark smoke," which Scottish explorer Alexander Mackenzie first described in 1793.

> When we had passed the last river, we observed smoke rising from it, as if produced by fires that had been freshly lighted. I therefore concluded that there were natives on its banks. We saw smoke rising in columns from many parts of the woods.

For communicating with his own men, Mackenzie soon came to rely on signal fire techniques learned from the locals. For his own sanity he also adopted their habit of lighting smoke-rich smudge fires to keep down the occasional scourge of mosquitoes and blackflies.

The northern fire masters of old used the tool of fire as we would a multiheaded screwdriver. They used fire to flush game animals, dry out trails and celebrate special events. They used it to thaw snow or frozen ground so they could collect berries, medicinal herbs or long strands of spruce root. They used it to build and patch the birchbark canoes so absolutely essential to their livelihood, an impossible task without fire-heated spruce gum. Sometimes they deliberately blazed old decadent forests near their camps to reduce dangerous fuel loads and lower the risk of much larger uninvited fires running them off the land. According to Stephen Janzen, they even used fire as a divining tool to improve hunting success.

> Near Fort Resolution, caribou hunters are known to have built fires where trails forked—one fire close to one trail and a second near the other. After the fires

had burnt down, the hunters would choose the lucky trail by noting the pile of burnt remains which best resembled caribou tracks.

So harnessed, fire gave early natives a real measure of control over their forest home and its resources, while distancing them as much as fate would allow from the worst of wildfires' whims. Like the cornered black bear or the fast-rising rapids, fire occasionally would turn on native people with sometimes devastating results. But, as one fire historian noted, "fire and nomadism were mutual causes and effects." Mobility was their antidote to the most destructive side of forest fires. Without stooping to the anthropological sin of creating (or recreating) the so-called ecologically noble savage, Henry Lewis concluded that the purposeful wielding of fire by the original inhabitants of this land "was simply part of a sound strategy for adaptation in a northern boreal forest."

CONFRONTING FIRE

For most European visitors to the North, fire wore a very different face. Rather than being a gift to humankind, as Prometheus would have it and as native people generally lived it, fire was largely a menace. It was destructive and wasteful, a potential threat to the storehouse of furs and food that the forest represented to them. Writing from his leather-backed chair in 1826, a Hudson's Bay Company officer at Fort Chipewyan wrote with some astonishment that there were "fires in every direction." There was no doubt in his mind about how they started. "These Chipewyans, I can't imagine what prepossession has now taken hold of them, blazing the Country in this manner." Inevitably some of the native-set fires did get out of hand. Many people attributed all fires to them. The French missionary Emile Petitot, who toured the region in the 1860s, left us another classic example of this kind of thinking. He concluded that every charred forest he came across was the result of "the savage's carelessness." After gloomily observing a burn near Great Bear Lake, he commented that the Dene were "insane" to destroy their land in such a way. Setting his biases aside momentarily, he did admit that traveling through burned country was often a whole lot easier than through spruce-choked woods.

> If dry wood becomes scarce, the Indian does not hesitate a moment, he sacrifices beauty to necessity, by setting fire to the forest. The fire will spread over the land, will ravage the country for many leagues. Little cares he. "What a beautiful country," he will cry some years after, "it can be traversed without the branches putting out your eyes, and we will have plenty to warm us for a long time."

In 1888 geological surveyor Robert Bell took an entirely different view. He proclaimed that fires in northern Canada were on the rise thanks to intruding Europeans. Bell believed that "the careless Indian" dwelled mostly in the imagination of people like Petitot, and he went to great lengths to dispel the notion altogether by turning over the coin. He maintained that it was matches struck by the hands of wandering newcomers that started most of the so-called anthropogenic fires.

> He very often avails himself of this easy means to make a smudge to keep off the mosquitoes, to light his pipe, dropping the burning match, or to make a little fire in order to boil his kettle and refresh himself with

a hot drink. The number of fire-setting travelers has greatly increased in comparatively recent times. These include fur traders, missionaries, surveyors, explorers, prospectors and, nearer to civilization, railway builders, common-road makers, lumbermen, bush-rangers and settlers.

Stephen Janzen picks up on Bell's thread and adds that "the migrant cared little if his fire burned the forests of an area he would never pass through again. The boreal forest's breathtaking size curbed man's interest in making sure the fire was out. This particular side effect of Canadian geography afflicted Indian and European alike."

When ripe for a burn, the forest made no distinction between sparks that escaped from a native or European campfire. It was no coincidence that some of the largest northern forest fires of the late nineteenth century sprang up along the most well-traveled rivers, lake shores and cross-country trails. While floating down the Mackenzie River on a mapping expedition, Robert Bell witnessed several monster fires and penned this searing account into his field book.

When the fire has got under way the pitchy trees burn with almost explosive rapidity. The flames rush through their branches and high above their tops with a terrifying sound. The ascending heat soon develops a strong breeze, if a wind does not happen to be blowing already. Before this gale the fire sweeps on with a roaring noise as fast as a horse can gallop. The irresistible front of a flame devours the forest before it as rapidly as a prairie fire licks up the dry grass. The line of the gigantic conflagration has a height of 100 feet or more above the treetops, or 200 feet from the ground.

Great sheets of flame disconnect themselves from the
fiery avalanche and leap upwards as towering tongues
of fire, or dart forward bridging over wide spaces, such
as lakes and rivers, and starting the fire afresh in
advance of the main column.

By the late 1880s questions were being asked about the
impact of such big fires on barren-ground caribou, the staple
food prized by natives and transplants alike. Hundreds of
thousands of these "buffalo of the tundra" depended, as they
still do, on the northern fringe of the boreal forest for winter
survival. For the first time in decades, fur traders, natives and
missionaries waited in vain for the caribou to arrive.
According to Corporal Arthur Mellor of the Royal North-
West Mounted Police, "The Indians were practically all starving, owing to the entire absence of caribou. Father Toure, the
priest there, informed me that this is the only time the deer
have failed to arrive, during his 42 year stay at the place." Was
the caribou decline due to disruptions of their winter range
by widespread fires? This was the conclusion reached by
Warburton Pike, who, on a hunting trip near Great Slave
Lake in 1889, was struck by the absence of caribou.

They [now] keep a more easterly route. This is in
great measure accounted for by the fact that great
stretches of the country have been burnt, and so rendered incapable of growing the lichen so dearly
beloved by these animals. The same thing applies at
Fort Resolution, where, within the last decade, the
southern shore of Great Slave Lake has been burnt and
one of the best ranges totally destroyed.

The nineteenth century ended in a blaze of northern forest fires, many of them caused by runaway campfires. During the peak of the Klondike Gold Rush in 1898 an incredible amount of forest was burned. That summer alone about a thousand gold seekers swarmed into the Yukon via Edmonton and the Northwest Territories, the so-called Canadian back door. They ventured down the Slave and Mackenzie rivers, then up the Liard, the Keele or the Peel and onward to the Yukon gold fields. In their wake they left an alarming trail of smoke and flames. Geologist Charles Camsell described a veritable sea of burned-over forests dating from that era. His notes suggest that he was seemingly forever in "an area of burnt rolling country."While doing surveys along the well-traveled Salt River valley near Fort Smith, one burn so impressed him that he felt compelled to climb the highest hill he could find to try to comprehend the fire's vast footprint. He glassed around with his binoculars, took a few bearings with his compass, then scribbled more in his field book: "I may say, that this area extends for a distance of 25 to 30 miles from north-east to south-west and runs as far to the north-west and south-east as could be seen from the tops of the hills."

Once the gold-seekers arrived in the Yukon they set off an explosion of forest fires. One witness to the fires of 1898–99 recorded this description: "At night campfires were visible in almost any direction one could look. The moss and brush by this time had become very dry, and as a result of the carelessness of campers in leaving their fires, forest fires began to rage along the valleys."

Prospectors and miners commonly lit fires to clear camps and hunt for placer gold. They burned cord after cord of split wood to melt down through the frozen ground, to take the *perma* out of *permafrost,* gradually penetrating the top layers of soil until they reached placer tills or bedrock. Nobody bothered to record the number of fires that escaped from these primitive operations. Plenty likely.

Nowadays a prospector can turn to aerial electromagnetics (using torpedolike "birds" slung below a helicopter), satellite images and computer models to get an understanding of hidden geological features and read their clues. In the old days prospectors sometimes gained this knowledge with the strike of a match. To many the forest was simply an inconvenient covering that masked the rock below. Historian Arthur Lower observed that some prospectors regarded the forest as an enemy to get rid of: "The prospector sees in the forest simply a covering preventing his knowing what kind of rock is under his feet." Commenting on a northern prospector's work in the Peel River region in 1898, another writer observed that "prospecting for this stuff [gold-bearing quartz] means hunting veins through the rock with pick and dynamite, after having first burned down the forest to let the surface of the rock be seen."

SKIRMISHING WITH FIRE

The first recorded efforts to stem tide of northern fires date back to the early 1800s. Both the Hudson's Bay Company and the upstart Nor'Westers viewed fire as a great threat to the business of trapping and trading furs. Setting up shop in the northwest was no cheap affair. They saw fire as a lurking peril ready to devour the huge amounts of capital invested in their isolated trading posts. Huge caches of furs, painstakingly gathered food supplies, precious tools and equipment, and the post buildings themselves all lay vulnerable to the ravages of fire. The fur traders' fears were fueled amply when a series of catastrophic fires struck northern Saskatchewan in the fall of 1813. They maintained that these fires disrupted commercial trade routes, decimated local animal populations and seriously weakened fur returns throughout the region. Two springs later the *Carlton House Journal* reported that the "country all around" and "for a considerable distance" was ablaze. Men worked around the clock to stop fire from "communicating with the works." Owning up to the fact that posts themselves were a potential source of ignition, company officials across the North were encouraged to clear flammable rubbish from buildings, keep copious supplies of water handy, patrol any fires that might sweep near the post and, when deemed sufficiently urgent, go out and battle the flames with everything they had.

In May 1832 western Canada's first fire regulations were proclaimed by the Council of Assiniboia. Their aim was to halt "the great injury done to the Woods of the Settlement by fire." To "check this evil" settlers were prohibited from lighting fires on their properties between February and December. Punishment for noncompliance was a stiff ten-pound fine.

Almost seventy years passed before the Canadian government made any real commitment to administering, if not controlling, fire in the "Great Northern Belt." Federal forestry took a brisk jump forward with the birth of the Dominion Forestry Branch in 1900. Chief Superintendent of Forestry Elihu Stewart had a consuming interest in forest fires. He had read the vivid testimonies of Robert Bell and others who described the awesome sweep of fire in the distant northern woodlands. One spring day in 1906 Stewart cleared off his desk, packed his bags and stepped onto a westbound train out of Ottawa. His chosen mission was to evaluate the worth of northern timber stocks and see firsthand how fire fit into the equation. A few weeks later he was steaming down the Mackenzie and up the Yukon shaking his head.

The spectacle witnessed by the traveler passing through our unsettled forest country is sad indeed. On every hand he beholds the charred remains of the old time forest. Everywhere this destruction of public property is before his eyes, and it is humiliating to confess, as we must do, that the fires which caused this great loss were not only permitted but in most cases caused by our own people.

Stewart returned to Ottawa with a firm resolve to protect what was left of the northern forest. Besides barren and blackened forests, he observed impressive stands of riparian spruce trees that in girth and height could rival those growing much farther south. In his report Stewart linked today's preservation of subarctic spruce to tomorrow's demands for pulpwood. He stressed the role of northern forests as a nursery for valuable fur-bearing animals. He concluded that it was government's legitimate role to take "responsibility of preventing as far as possible these virgin forests from meeting the fate that has overtaken those in more frequented parts." Foremost in his mind were the once great white pine stands of central Canada, most of which, even by Stewart's day, had fallen to unrestrained fires and axes.

Enter the northern fire ranger. Who was this man? He was the spearhead of Stewart's policy to protect the northern forest. He was the enforcer of Ottawa's new fire regulations. He was a teacher and part-time evangelist spreading the good name of fire prevention. Understandably the fire ranger's role in actually stomping out forest fires in progress was largely symbolic. Here's how his job description read in 1912:

A fire-ranger in these northern districts must be able to speak the native languages, and must be an expert in a canoe and among horses. He must know a very larger tract of country like a book, for on many occasions he is called upon to make long trips inland from the rivers, where there are no trails to follow or blazes to guide him.

Swiftness of movement was essential for the fire-ranger out on patrol. "The important feature is to get around the beat as quickly as possible and consequently be on the scene of a fire before it attains serious proportions."

How was the fire ranger to achieve this swiftness? By canoe or by steam-powered paddle-wheeler? This was a moot question tossed around by staff at the forestry operations headquarters in Fort Smith. Some felt that a fleet of canoes represented the best means of fire ranging. Canoes could take a ranger virtually anywhere in the well-watered North and provided easy access to the shore when a fire might need quick attention. Those in the steamer school asserted that boats under power were far better for going upriver and could carry more men and equipment to work on a fire.

What the steamer advocates neglected to stress was the fact that some of the most valuable stands of northern spruce were being chopped down to feed hungry boilers in steamboats, including those owned and operated by the forestry department. Their newest, fastest steamers burned no less than two cords of wood every hour. That's a pile of wood taking up as much space as a good-sized log cabin designed to comfortably sleep twelve men. Furthermore those very boats represented a roving source of fire ignition. One observer wrote of the "distressing wrack and ruin" caused by steamers chugging up and down the treelined northern waterways. "As soon as the boat has loaded up and forced draught is put on in order to get the boat off shore, incandescent fragments of cinders are vomited out of the funnels into the woods with disastrous consequences."

Sparks or no sparks, forestry officials finally reached a simple compromise on how fire rangers should range. They decreed that the canoe would be the chief means for them to travel downstream. On specific dates they were to meet the steamer to pick up fresh supplies and instructions or climb aboard for the journey back upstream.

During most summers there were less than a dozen fire rangers plying the waters of the Mackenzie District, an area about the size of France and Spain combined. In practical terms the best these few men could hope to achieve in this immense landscape was a reduction in fire starts along well-traveled waterways. Once in the field some no doubt felt paralyzed by the absurdity of this task. Others took a more easy-going approach, availing themselves of numerous "small excursions to visit friends in the neighborhood." Still others carried out their duties with apparent valor and steadfast loyalty to the cause, at least so a *Saturday Evening Post* article would have it.

A thousand miles north of the British line one has seen a fire guardian, the only officer of his kind in a section of country hundreds of miles in extent. . . . A splendid, quiet self-respecting chap this man was too. . . . One day during a steamer voyage this fire guardian saw smoke on the horizon far inland from the river on which we were traveling. He stopped the boat at once, got his pack together and went ashore. As he figured it out, this fire was forty miles away. . . . All alone, a sturdy self-reliant figure—representing the law, representing civilization even in the wilderness, representing a decent regard of the organized society that is to follow

us—he set out on foot for his wilderness journey
across an untracked country. In all of one's experience
with outdoor men, rarely has one met a better and
nobler figure than this one.

The northern fire ranger, however capable, faced challenges that were nothing short of Herculean. His "greatest
handicaps," says Janzen, "were created by the north's cruel
geography and almost insurmountable distances. . . . Few
places on earth have such an impenetrable expanse of forest,
where land dwarfs transportation corridors so absolutely." In
1915 a lone ranger was strapped with the task of patrolling the
area from Fort Smith north to Fort Resolution plus the
country adjacent to Great Slave Lake and all its tributaries, of
which there are scores. For good measure his boss threw in
the land embracing the Mackenzie River all the way to Fort
Providence. Among the other "unique difficulties" cited by
Janzen were "poor communication, inconsistent transportation, and the matter of introducing natives to the foreign
concept of fire regulations."

This latter task—peddling and enforcing laws that banned
any use of fire beyond basic cooking and heating—was a particularly delicate business. This rubbed against the cultural
grain of local fire practices that reached back through millennia. Torching the forest to modify animal habitats, create
firewood or improve access; lighting one smoky fire after
another to keep the bugs down or signal a neighboring hunting party—these practices were now taboo. A Chipewyan
buffalo hunter who lived off the land near Fort Smith voiced
his confusion created by this clash of cultural values. "We
burned the meadows to keep them clear of poplar, every
spring while there was still snow in the bush. But we had to
stop, before I was twenty even."

What made enforcement even trickier, says Janzen, was the fact that "many seasonal rangers made their homes in the area and could ill-afford to have themselves ostracized in an environment where one's survival could depend on the goodwill of neighbors." Consequently the hand of frontier justice usually came down lightly on local heads. After investigating several human-caused fires during the 1915 season, one ranger defended his style of proper punishment: "The penalties imposed in the cases tried were light, and the object was rather to prevent carelessness for the future than to punish for the past." Besides burning bridges among neighbors, if the ranger wielded too firm a hand he risked sparking "retaliatory fires." Someone unhappy about how fire regulations were enforced might decide to light a fire out of spite, safe in the knowledge that in such a huge landscape getting caught was next to impossible.

T.W. Harris was among those fire rangers who took great pride in their work. He felt gratified that the seeds of fire prevention he helped sow had taken root. In 1915 he informed his supervisors, "the more intelligent among the Indians are beginning to be convinced that the preventative measures are for the good of the country, and are willing to cooperate with us if they can do so without seriously compromising themselves with the other Indians." In 1919 some of Harris's co-workers returned to the Mackenzie region after a long absence and were pleased to report that "the waste by fire is by no means as great now, and the natives are being educated to see the folly of allowing fires to spread." Such testimonies may well point to one of the more astonishing ambitions of federal forestry: to convince an entire culture to make a complete about-face in its views on fire in less than two decades. On the other hand such testimonies might have been somewhat embellished in the interests of promoting job security. For it was not long afterward that the heads of many a northern fire ranger began to roll.

John A. McDougal was a senior official with the forest service who in 1923 had very little good to say about the fire ranger program. He saw no worth in northern timber, certainly not enough to justify the expense of patrol work. "In my opinion," he wrote, "it is a waste of money to carry on the fire ranging system on a scale carried on during the past few years. Owing to the vastness of the District, unless a fire ranger was fortunate enough to be at the spot when a fire started or to arrive in time to prevent it spreading, he would have difficulty securing assistance to fight a fire owing to the scarcity of the population." McDougal was a realist. He was also a pragmatist. Less than a year after bashing the fire ranger program he was offered a job as chief fire ranger. Without a qualm he gladly accepted the position and proceeded to erase the names of all northern fire rangers from the government payroll list, including one T.W. Harris. From now on, proclaimed McDougal, the job of waving the flag of fire prevention could jolly well be left to the RCMP—that is, when they weren't busy with real police work.

And so it was that for the next twenty years, unhampered by the meagre protection imposed by the RCMP, nature had her way as fires continued to ebb and flow freely through the northern forest. The number of fires reached a peak in the late 1920s, when much of the region south of Great Slave Lake was on fire. In 1929 a fire covering over fifty square kilometers almost engulfed the town of Fort Smith. Fires in Wood Buffalo National Park burned so far and wide that Warden D'Arcy Arden seriously considered kicking all trappers, native and white, out of the park to help prevent more conflagrations. "The whole country is on fire," he wrote, adding that "fire came like hell." A pilot for Western Canada

Airways reported with dismay that the south end of the Park was "nearly all burned away." Bad press from the *Edmonton Journal*—"this will seriously hurt the next few years' fur catch"—and a sympathetic forestry administrator named O.S. Finnie almost prompted a renaissance of the ill-fated fire ranger program. But the Depression quashed Finnie's plans. Janzen writes that "support for forest conservation had dwindled throughout Canada since the mid-1920s and was one of the first victims of economic retrenchment."

Even as the Depression kept its stranglehold on much of the nation, northern Canada's first mine was opening on the shore of Great Bear Lake's McTavish Arm. By the summer of 1933 Eldorado Mines was making regular shipments of uranium and silver concentrate to markets in southern Canada and the United States. That same year mapping work by the Geological Survey of Canada identified some mighty interesting mineral prospects in the neighborhood of Yellowknife Bay. The flurry of prospecting that followed climaxed in September 1935, when Fred Jolliffe and his party of greenhorn geologists discovered the gold that put Yellowknife on the map. As another flood of gold seekers headed north Jolliffe remarked that "probably there were more prospectors in this area in 1938 than any other part of Canada." As the miners and prospectors spread across the northland in growing numbers, so did forest fires, among the worst on record. Many of the region's contemporary forests took root in the wake of fires dating back to the 1930s.

The fires carried on into the 1940s with no ebb in sight. True to the established pattern of spasmodic northern development, there suddenly arrived a new actor on the stage with matches in hand: the United States military. In northern British Columbia and the Yukon, military troops building the Alaska Highway were wreaking havoc upon the forests through their careless fire practices. Meanwhile forests in the Northwest Territories were suffering at the hands of thousands of military personnel bent on stringing a road and oil pipeline across the Mackenzie Mountains, the Canol Line, and scattering air-staging bases across the North. One observer commented that "it seems to be the opinion of the troops to let the country burn, it's no good anyway." Northern fires during the war years were serious enough to merit the attention of then Minister of Mines and Resources T.A. Crerar. In 1943 he wrote an ironic note to his American counterpart reminding him that "the only force available to suppress fires started along the transportation routes is that controlled by the United States engineers." One of the largest fires ever recorded in North America spread from unburned slash piled recklessly along the Alaska Highway in the southern Yukon. By the fall of 1942 this one fire had consumed an area of forest the size of Ireland, burning as far east as the Mackenzie River, which it reportedly jumped near Fort Simpson.

While visiting the region in 1942, Malcolm Macdonald, a dignitary from Ottawa, reported that "fires galore" had been raging all summer. "Consequently, a thick pall of smoke, as dense as a bad fog, has hung over the whole country between Edmonton and Great Slave Lake week after week, at a time when air and river transport is usually very active. For long periods, every airplane in the place has been grounded, and small craft like scows have been tied up." It got so bad at times that airports as far south as Edmonton occasionally shut down due to sky-filling smoke that wafted down from the Northwest Territories.

Western Canadians were demanding relief from the chronic palls of northern smoke. Grounded pilots from Edmonton to Yellowknife were pacing the hangars in frustration. Biologists fond of the North went public with their concerns over rampant fires. Dr. C.H.D. Clarke's field reports from the southwestern Northwest Territories predicted local extinctions of woodland caribou caused by destructive fires in their rangeland. The Hudson's Bay Company joined in the fray by repeating their decades-old refrain that unchecked fires were ruining the fur trade. But the loudest complaints came from the mining community, which was fast overtaking furs as the Northwest Territories' number one industry. Devastating timber losses near Great Slave Lake in 1944 prompted *The Northern Miner* to run an article demanding immediate action against forest fires: "The loss of such timber in an area that could be easily patrolled by airplane is a rebuke to the administration." The article concluded that "having in mind the ultimate demand which is certain to develop for mine timbers, the government should commence immediately to provide the necessary equipment and organization to promptly deal with fires as they arise next year." All kinds of interest groups were turning up the heat on the federal government to start controlling fire in the northern forest, an environment that, as yet, had refused to be tamed. Were the feds now up to the task?

"No funds! No funds! No funds!" was all some Ottawa bureaucrats could say in response. Given their commitment to help sponsor a world war, this was an understandable though regrettable reply. One forestry spokesman, Harry Holman, admitted realistically that blanket fire protection for the North was out of the question. But Holman was a "man of obvious conviction" and added that "at the same time we have got to recognize that something must be done, and at once, if we are to hold down losses even to what they have been. With each added activity in the north, the danger mounts." Less easy to swallow was the response offered by forestry administrators in Fort Smith. According to Stephen Janzen, they defended their

> impotent protection efforts by reasoning that the fire difficulties arose from the activities of the very people most willing to criticize: careless prospectors—some of whom [still] intentionally set fire so as to expose rock formations; Indians, who resented the fact that development was taking place on native game preserves; mining companies that desired fire-killed wood as a cheap form of fuel; and aircraft companies that set fires in the hopes of drumming up business.

From pleas of poverty and open-ended promises to trenchant accusations, the collective response of the federal government translated into one clear recommendation: "For now, we'll have to stand back and let the fires burn."

DECLARING WAR ON FIRE

The feds sang a radically different tune soon after the war ended. It was with genuine postwar gusto that they launched a flurry of initiatives and threw pot after pot of money at developing the North. As if waking from a long slumber they looked afresh at the top of their dominion and remembered the minerals, remembered the oil and remembered the "untouched stands of merchantable timber." They remembered also the looming shadows cast by their American and Russian brethren and looked askance at their undefended, barely proclaimed northern boundaries. It was time, they thought, for more authoritative policies to exploit, control and protect their northern storehouse of riches. And to safeguard their investment in northern roads, railways, settlements and equipment—not to mention the timber—it was time to get organized and get tough on forest fires.

Twenty years after the fire ranger program was fleeced, the feds put fire control back on their northern agenda. They established an entirely new arm of government, the Forest and Wildlife Division of the Northwest Territories, charged with managing forests, fire and furs. Annual operating costs for fire prevention and combat took off from day one and quickly broke one hundred thousand dollars. The first superintendent of the division was E.G. Oldham. On the day he took office he resolved to bury the legacy of recent fires in the Mackenzie District. Oldham calculated that 50 per cent of the area's forests had been destroyed by fire from 1940 to 1945. He made protection of game animals in the unburned forests his primary goal on one condition: that he be granted the wherewithal to protect the forests from further devastation. "The most thorough and accurate wildlife surveys possible can be completed," he told his masters in the Northwest Territories Council, "but if protection is disregarded and uncontrolled fires sweep the country [there will be] little to conserve or manage."

Though many forest fires burned out of control summer after summer, fire management capabilities continued to grow on several fronts. During each fire season, a crew of field-trained fire fighters was kept on constant call in most of the larger communities. New patrol boats, Jeeps, tractors and other support vehicles were shipped up from the south. Axes, portable pumps, fuel and other fire-fighting equipment were cached strategically throughout the region. Numerous small aircraft were chartered to help with fire detection and aerial reconnaissance work. Floatplanes and, later, helicopters were used to ferry men and supplies to the fire fronts. Back in the Fort Smith command center, statistics were carefully logged on fires burned, fires "actioned," weather conditions, supplies and aircraft used and, on the bottom line, dollars spent. The 1946 report summarizing the Forest and Wildlife Division's maiden year documented fifty-eight fires that burned almost 610,000 hectares of trees. Northerners were beginning to enjoy a new source of income: fire money, they called it.

On the prevention side of fire management, Oldham took two major steps forward. He made enforcement and education top priorities. He introduced a forest protection ordinance that gave forest officers sweeping powers, including permission to arrest without warrant anyone causing a forest fire through negligence or worse. A grander and friendlier initiative was his broad "publicity offensive," which he launched in 1950. Hundreds of letters explaining the do's and don'ts of fire prevention poured out of the Fort Smith office. They were addressed to mining companies, sawmill operators, business organizations, schools and community leaders. Fire officials asked residents and visitors to the Mackenzie District to cooperate in detecting, reporting and, where possible, suppressing fires with their own two hands. They asked church leaders and school teachers to help in the good fight against fires by "teaching the lessons of good citizenship." They gave lectures, posted signs and sponsored ads in local newspapers and radio networks warning the public about the menace of fire. They toured the communities, small and smaller, firing up the community hall generators to show educational films on forest conservation to full-house audiences. Favorite hits included *Tomorrow's Timber*, *Temagami Ranger* and *Forest Commandos*. After two years of blitzing the public, fire officials measured the success of their prevention campaign by the number of people who had the book thrown at them. In 1952 they were proud to report only nine new convictions due to fire law infractions.

Now that northern fires were being systematically observed, if not always controlled, fire personnel noticed over the years that no two fire seasons were alike. Each developed its individual signature determined by the dryness and species composition of the forests, the temperature and humidity of the air, the strength and direction of the winds, the severity and extent of thunderstorms, and the number of humans sitting around campfires or chain-smoking in the bush. Some seasons were a breeze with frequent rains dousing most fires before they got too big. Other seasons transformed the northern forest into a war zone.

To compare fighting fire to fighting a war is only natural. Both depend on the capability to thwart the opponent's chances of surprise attack, to keep a constant surveillance on its activities and movements, and to send at any moment highly trained forces plus massive amounts of equipment and supplies to the front lines of battle. Words like *onslaught*, *attack* and *retreat* became commonplace in the growing stacks of annual fire reports written after a burn was declared officially out.

One of the worst fire seasons on record came in 1950. Burned into the memory of any front-line fighters still alive is the dreaded Point Ennuyuese Fire. In less than two days it roared over fifty kilometers up the Slave River valley, stopping just short of the very home of the North's fire-fighting nerve center, Fort Smith. Aided by a sudden shift in winds from north to south, a well-organized suppression crew from town was able to beat down and contain the southern front of the fire. Meanwhile other crews were dispatched to the northern line of fire, where they patrolled the massive flame front by boat, barge, tractor and foot. The awful campaigns waged and won that summer were judged by Harry Holman, a visiting forester from Ottawa, as very hopeful signs of progress. He declared that "the fire suppression set-up here will eventually become as efficient as anywhere." Headquarters showed good judgment, he thought, in deciding first which fires should be fought, and then when and how. Holman knew full well that like a doctor treating wartime combat victims on the field of battle such decisions were not easy. In his wrap-up report he wrote that "it must be realized that in an area as large as this, every fire cannot be fought, for if one attempted to do so, fire suppression would mount into astronomical figures."

The mettle of Fort Smith fire officials got its biggest test ever in the mid-1950s. In 1953 a handful of spot fires in northern Alberta quickly blew up into major fires that merged somewhere south of Hay River, then threatened to engulf the town. Strong southwest winds fanned the flames, spreading them as far east as the Slave River valley. In the fire's path were several small settlements and some of the best timber North of Sixty. That same summer another fire, Number 41, burst out of Wood Buffalo National Park on a front over thirty kilometers wide. It staggered dangerously close to the community of Fort Fitzgerald, then as if judging its prey too small, suddenly swung north towards Fort Smith. Benevolent winds and quick-witted fire-fighting efforts saved all threatened communities and the best of the timber. The operation was subsequently dubbed "an excellent exercise in civil defense." The year 1956 on the other hand was a good one for fires and a lousy one for fire suppression. Hardest hit was the middle Mackenzie Valley. During the peak of the fire season the Forest Service's Superintendent R.T. Flanagan took a smoky reconnaissance flight over the area to see for himself how bad it was. "I remember flying down the Mackenzie with my boss from Ottawa. We were going just past Fort Norman and a goddamn big smoke started coming up on the west side of the Mackenzie River, and he looked at that and said, 'What d'ya gonna do with that fire?' I said, 'I'm gonna take a picture of it.' And that's all we did, that's all we could do."

During big fire years like 1956, many native trappers became hot under the collar as they watched flames reduce their livelihood to ashes by destroying traditional trapping areas. Back country cabins, long-established hunting camps and valued big game habitats also fell victim to wildfires. The district administrator in Fort Smith, L.A. Hunt, offered his sympathies to those who had suffered losses. He told his superiors that the loss of trapping areas in particular posed a serious economic threat and hoped that future funding increases would lead to "fairly large-scale coverage." He posed the question: "Are we to continue the present meagre policy which does very little in any case to protect the forests from destruction?"

Pressure to further extend the long arm of fire protection mounted when, yet again, the caribou question raised its head. Hunters, biologists and southern conservationists voiced their concerns over the impact of far-reaching fires on the winter range of this still-coveted species. They claimed that forest fires were among the caribou's worst enemies. They claimed that caribou were starving to death in parts of their range because of the widespread destruction of lichens, one of caribou's primary foods. Abundant fuel was added to their arguments in the early 1960s, when a series of intense fires burned a two-million-hectare hole in the caribou winter range lying between Great Bear and Great Slave lakes.

What impact did this have on these animals? Did it cause their numbers to decline? Was their migration subsequently deflected to other areas? No one could ever say for sure. But without doubt those fires set the alarm bells ringing as far south as Ottawa. Digging deep in their pockets with one hand and crossing their fingers with the other, members of Treasury Board unearthed special funds to increase northern fire protection. In 1965 the caribou lobby got their reserve. All fires would now be actioned automatically in what became known simply as the Caribou Range, a 111,000-square-kilometer area of spruce–lichen woodland south of Fort Reliance and east of Fort Smith. This apparent handout dazzled the northern public, who in turn clamored for more. Their pleas for greater coverage were greeted with repeated reminders that fire protection must remain within the limits of practicality. "All we can hope to do in protecting this northern country," stated one official, "is offset the effect of human activity, and we may consider ourselves very fortunate if we are able to do that."

In 1966 Fort Smith declared war on close to two hundred fires that covered a total of 350,000 square kilometers, or a land area about the size of Germany. This represented almost one quarter of the Mackenzie District's enormous land base. An imposing arsenal was pressed into service to wage the summer's many battles. Headquarters staff mobilized a rapid deployment force of native fire fighters stationed from one end of the district to the other. All command and control functions were coordinated via a system of new detection towers, field camps and a state-of-the-art telecommunications network. Fort Smith's growing inventory of heavy equipment now included long-range aircraft with water bombing capabilities. Armed with the latest fire-fighting techniques, crews flew out to remote corners of the district on the coattails of lightning storms, often detecting and extinguishing fires before they had a chance to catch a breath. All this brought operating costs to about half a million dollars a year.

For historian Stephen Janzen there was a kind of panache about spending these kinds of big bucks on frontier wildfires. "While certainly expensive, the ability to suppress back-country fires made it undeniably seductive." Panache or no, the purse-holders in Ottawa became increasingly skeptical about the wisdom of an ever-expanding blanket of fire protection for areas of "little or no value." As if to prove out these worries the feds emptied their fire coffers fully, and then some, in the wake of the record-busting fires of 1968 and 1971.

In early August of 1968, Fire Number 34 raced toward the recently established "model town" of Inuvik. Fire records describe it as "probably the most serious ever experienced in the Mackenzie District, in that it presented a very real and serious threat to a major community." Military Hercules planes and other large aircraft stood by on red alert status in anticipation of a speedy evacuation of the entire town. Over the course of several anxious days the fire ballooned to cover 35,200 hectares of tree-line forest. Four hundred men were flown in to do battle with the flames. This represented most of the available fire fighters in the Northwest Territories plus a troop of special reserves sent up from northern Alberta. It was the most intensive suppression campaign ever mounted North of Sixty, and in the end it was a success. Ray Schmidt, who gave over three decades of his life to the Mackenzie Forest Service, had never seen a far northern fire like Number 34: "Until someone devised a hazard rating which used the comparative and the superlative of extreme, like 'extremer' and 'extremest,' there would be no real description of what the unrelieved midnight sun could do to the forest fuels at those high latitudes."

The 1971 season was labeled by some as a complete disaster. Fire costs skyrocketed to five million as 322 fires burned

A water bomber's efforts to douse a treeline fire is hampered by dense smoke. (Photo: Government of Northwest Territories Archives)

an estimated 930,800 hectares. Evacuation tactics almost used on Inuvik three summers earlier were almost used on the town of Pine Point, which lay for some days in the path of a monster fire. That summer took the lives of two men, who were killed on the fire line by falling snags. Another four died the next week in an aircraft accident. While circling in dense smoke above a crashed helicopter (the pilot of which survived), two CANSO water bombers collided head on, killing all crew members on board. Stephen Hume, a journalist visiting the Fort Smith fire center, wrote a gripping account of the havoc played by forest fires that summer.

> The huge wall map of the Northwest Territories bristled with colored pins—bright red for active fires, yellow for suspected but unconfirmed fires, black, appropriately, for burned out fires. I counted 263 of the red and yellow pins, and new ones were being added.

On the wall next to the maps were charts which indicated falling humidity and the nearly total absence of water in the environment. The fire control officer had bigger problems than supply and demand. He explained that when the electrical storms scattered the fires across his district in such numbers he had cannibalized the Yellowknife Fire District on the north side of Great Slave Lake. Now, that zone had its own outbreak of serious fires. One had cut the Mackenzie Highway—Yellowknife's only land link to the outside world—and knocked out power from the town's hydroelectric plant on the Snare River. The territorial capital was getting by with emergency power from a diesel generator.

GOVERNING FIRE

Political fallout from the 1971 fire debacles rained down heavily on the Mackenzie Forest Service. Treasury Board officials in Ottawa were astounded by the exorbitant cost (they hadn't seen anything yet) of protecting what most of them considered to be useless forest. The destruction of prime wildlife habitat angered native people, who felt that most aerial and ground combat against fires had been waged in areas valued only by industrial society. One group of vocal trappers was so incensed that they hopped on a plane and took their complaints about inadequate fire protection directly to the Prime Minister's Office. The message from all sides was clear: it was time to completely overhaul the way fire-fighting decisions were made.

Two unremarkable fire seasons came and went. Then out of the pipeline of paper from Ottawa came not more money but a name change for northern forestry operations—the

*A CANSO water bomber attempts to stem the fiery tide by drop-
ping thousands of liters of fire retardant along the flame front.*
(Photo: Government of Northwest Territories Archives)

Northern Lands and Forest Service—plus a spanking new
fire protection policy. Its stated objective was "to reduce forest fire damages to a level consistent with the present and
future needs of the people to ensure the continuation of their
enjoyment and use of the resources."

"Huh?" said the people.

"Look more closely at the policy," said the policy makers. The new policy divided the forested Northwest Territories into four zones on the basis of fire-fighting priority. Zones 1 and 2, the highest priorities, encompassed settlements, mines, tourist lodges, roads and prime timber areas. Important wildlife and trapping areas were assigned to Zone 3. The balance fell into Zone 4, where fires were at best watched from afar. Let nature have her way—that was the basic idea of Zone 4. "In remote areas, where protection of life and property is not required, the general aim," said the policy, "will be to limit fire damage to a level believed to have existed for thousands of years."

Though the fire policy was innovative, all parties soon came to agree on one point: It was practically impossible to implement fairly and squarely. For instance, why were so many well-known trapping areas abandoned to Zone 4? And what do we do with Zone 4 fires that sneak toward Zones 1, 2 or 3? And who decides whether or not a Zone 3 fire is actioned? One employee strapped with the task of putting the policy to work found himself having to wobble between a stance of "fighting all fires" to "fighting as few fires as possible." In a 1973 memo to Treasury Board, the deputy minister of Indian and Northern Affairs wrote that "hopefully by 1974, an extension of the protected area and additional funds will enable us to eliminate these problems." The feds were not in the mood to listen. The hem of the fire protection blanket was not lengthened, and additional funds never materialized. Nevertheless by 1976 annual fire costs were dragged over the three-million-dollar mark. The response from Ottawa took even the Fort Smith staff by surprise. They were ordered to *reduce* coverage by letting all fires burn in Zone 3 unless they posed an immediate threat to settlements. In effect this meant going back to the unsatisfactory status quo that ruled before the policy ever existed.

As smoke from the 1977 fire season began to rise so did public protests for more control over fire fighting. These were turbulent times in the North. A politically astute native youth movement was surfacing. New stirrings of self-determination were sparked by Justice Thomas Berger's Mackenzie Valley Pipeline Inquiry. The protests and demands boiled over amidst the unparalleled conflagrations of 1979. Janzen described this season as "tremendous by any standard." Beginning in early June "a seemingly endless array of large, expensive and destructive fires rolled across the southern forests of the NWT." By the end of the month, most of the fire-fighting resources were gone. July opened with paralyzing smoke that grounded most air operations and virtually shut down all fire detection activities. When the smoke cleared two months later, the tally came to 380 fires that burned over two million hectares. Disgruntled Dene natives demanded that the complex priority zone system for fighting fires be scrapped in favor of more direct control over the process. This time the government was listening. Local committees were formed in many communities to advise bureaucrats on fire management decisions. It turned out that in principle everyone wanted the same thing: "a fire management plan based on the needs of the people and involving them in its preparation." The Northwest Territories became the first region in North America to offer its inhabitants direct input on the where, when and how of wildfire management.

The ointment soon filled with flies as bureaucrats struggled to translate the *vox populi* into concrete fire management procedures. According to Janzen, "increasing public involvement was an admirable sentiment, but not altogether practical." The uncontrolled flames of 1979 had burned many bridges of trust between locals and those supposedly charged

Native fire fighters look twice before advancing upon a stubborn blaze in the Mackenzie valley. (PHOTO: GOVERNMENT OF NORTHWEST TERRITORIES ARCHIVES)

with protecting their interests. At the same time native activism was rising fast. In this heated political climate it became impossible to build a fire management policy by consensus. "Put simply," says Janzen, "the Dene viewed the policy-making process as a sham and wanted nothing less than complete control of the fire program." Given such control they would "be happy with nothing but a policy geared towards *complete fire exclusion.*" This from a people, who just a few generations ago had been baffled by the white man's revulsion to forest fires, a natural and formerly useful phenomenon that was as much a part of the land's fabric as the trees they burned.

Janzen describes this about-face on fire as one of "the most sweeping changes in the relationship between fire and man in the Canadian North." To the majority of natives a much valued ally to their traditional way of life was now an enemy. A circle in history closed. "Only fifty years earlier," says Janzen, "the bulk of the federal government's protection work involved trying to convince inhabitants of the same region to give up traditional fire practices in the hope of preventing fires. Within half a century, Ottawa's fire prevention and suppression efforts had completely reshaped native's traditional perception of fire." Janzen cites the death of nomadism as another potent force in shaping local attitudes about fire.

No longer could hunting communities simply move after fire had swept through their lands; they were settled. As a consequence, there grew a more pressing need for the protection of valuable habitat in areas surrounding communities lest they be completely destroyed by fire. Like most North Americans, inhabitants of the Northwest Territories had come to view fire as both unwanted and unnecessary.

During the nagging quest for an acceptable fire management policy, the federal government tasted some of its own medicine in much concentrated form and proclaimed that the dosage was too rich. The demand for complete and utter exclusion of fire from the northern forest was flatly unrealistic. What the people eventually got in 1983 was a much simplified policy that included a Fire Action Zone, the fluid boundaries of which would be determined through local consultations, and an Observation Zone, where fires would be . . . well . . . watched. In trying to sell their latest policy to an embittered public, fire officials added a new, almost revolutionary slant to the debate. They argued that some fires *should* be allowed to burn unmolested for the good of the forest. Besides decrying the soaring costs of northern fire fighting, they pointed to recent scientific studies that emphasized the need to "incorporate the role of fire in the northern environment." That fire was all very natural and normal and in fact needed came as news to some of those able to listen. They were told that if fire was totally excluded from the forest, mounting fuel loads over the years could turn it into a powder keg ready to blow up into fires more severe than any on record. Instead the aim was to manage fire in a way that mimicked what was believed to be the primeval fire regime: a combination of frequent light surface fires with the odd intense conflagration thrown into the mix. Anything less would deny fire its rightful place as both destroyer and sustainer of the northern forest.

This platform in the new fire policy introduced an ironic twist in the public relations work of fire managers. They were, concludes Janzen,

> suddenly faced with the tricky task of dispelling the notion—much vaunted by the fire organization since its conception—that forest fires were exclusively detrimental. The public had to be made aware that man influences the forest environment as much through successful fire exclusion as he does through increased fire activity.

When backed into a corner, the fire lords cut to the quick: "Fire: you can't live with it and you can't live without it."

LIVING WITH FIRE

In 1987 the federal government backed out of the northern fire fighting business altogether. To the Northwest Territories government that took over, they left behind their good wishes, a guaranteed but much debated multiyear budget and an arsenal of fire-detecting and -fighting technology that would make most of their provincial counterparts go green. The fire crew at the Fort Smith Fire Center were well acquainted with the science and strategies of fighting northern forest fires. They were equipped with electronic surveillance gear that could automatically track and record lightning storms over a thousand kilometers away. They had sophisticated meteorological forecasting equipment and the latest in computerized technology to analyze and map forest fire potentials and ongoing field campaigns. Standing by at the airport was a fleet of advanced fire-fighting aircraft, including a pair of Canadair CL-215 water bombers. Recognized across the forested north by its distinctive red belly, yellow wings and throaty window-shaking roar, this flying boat could scoop up close to six metric tons of water in ten seconds. In less than one second it could drop its entire payload onto a fire.

By the early 1990s the fire crew had the capability to track the size and movements of forest fires from an observation post eight hundred kilometers above the earth's surface. Fires veiled from airplane pilots by dense smoke could now be monitored daily using thermal images beamed down from the United States' NOAA satellite.

A special squadron of Turbo Firecats is recruited to assist the grow-ing arsenal of northern fire-fighting machines during a particularly tough summer. (Photo: Government Northwest Territories Archives)

Near the end of the summer of 1994 about all they could do was watch the fires burn. This was far and away the worst fire season recorded on any data base, stuffed in any files or lodged in anyone's memory: hot, dry and windy with lots of lightning storms—a pyromaniac's fantasy. It got so busy that three CANSO air tankers were called in from Saskatchewan to give air support to the overworked CL-215 sisters. They flew over fifty missions, all of them expensive, most of them dangerous. The helicopter budget bottomed out before the end of July. By late August action had been taken on over 450 fires—200 above average. At one point simultaneous fires covered an area four times the size of Prince Edward Island. The summer's fire-fighting bill to taxpayers was climbing fast toward—heaven forbid—the thirty-million-dollar mark.

The Fort Smith Fire Center was forced to remain on red alert status into the Labor Day holiday weekend. The head of fire operations, Dennis Mahussier, extended his sympathies to his exhausted crew when he broke the news in a hastily written memo: "Initial attack forces will be maintained throughout the weekend to the dismay of most fire personnel, and understandably so. Quite simply WE HAVE ALL HAD ENOUGH!" He tried to console them with his prayers for a change in the weather. "I never thought a four-letter word could be so revered—rain, rain, rain!"

It could be that we still ain't seen nothin' yet. The gap between record-breaking forest fire seasons is fast shrinking. It used to be measured in decades. Now, previous heights in dollars spent, fires fought or hectares torched are surpassed in a mere two or three years. Some boreal ecologists link this upward spiral of wildfires to the greenhouse effect, which, over the next fifty years, could raise the average temperature of subarctic summers by as much as five degrees Celsius. If the climate changes as predicted, more frequent and intense wildfires should come as no surprise thanks to drier forests, parched soils and a much-extended burning season. Atmospheric upheavals triggered by global warming promise more unstable, stormier weather for the North. This will mean increased lightning, which starts most forest fires, and more wind, which readily spreads them around. All this could spell a perilous upset in fire's ancient balancing act between destroying the boreal forest and rejuvenating it. In the next century—no matter how many fires are fought—the balance may well tip toward destruction.

In the meantime, come what may, the notion of "good" and "bad" fire years will persist, expressing our collective hopes and fears for the northern forest. Ultimately, the only sure thing we *can* control about forest fires is our attitude.

History tells us that however we view fire—as a wildlife management tool, an agent of forest renewal, a scourge on the land or a chronic threat to life and livelihood—there is wisdom in accepting that its signature, etched so deeply into the boreal forest, will always be written in Nature's hand, not ours.

BETWEEN A ROCK AND
A HARD PLACE

*This is an ancient transverse fault similar in character
to the Great Glen fault in Scotland and the San
Andreas fault in California. The main difference is
one of time, not character.*
—Ron Redfern, The Making of a Continent

Nothing invigorates a geologist more than a *bona fide*
earth-shaking event. "To see a glacier, witness an erup-
tion and feel an earthquake is the natural and legitimate
ambition of a properly constituted geologist," wrote G.K.
Gilbert, former chief of the United States Geological Survey.
Over a long career as a field geologist, Gilbert was fortunate
enough to witness these kinds of events many times over.
What he missed out on, though, by only a few hours, was the
monster earthquake along the San Andreas Fault that swallowed Matilda the cow. It happened in 1906. While the streets
of San Francisco reeled and buildings toppled, out at the
Shafter farm north of town the cow pasture was opening up.
In his report to the state commission investigating the earthquake, Gilbert described this peculiar event in no uncertain
terms: "In this connection mention may be made of the fact
that at the Shafter Ranch a fault crevice was momentarily so
wide as to admit a cow, which fell in head first and was thus
entombed. The closure which immediately followed left only
the tail visible.... At the time of my visit, the tail had disappeared, being eaten by dogs, but there was abundant testimo-
ny to substantiate the statement."

At the time of *my* visit to the Shafter Ranch ninety years later, little had changed. The cow pasture and bright red barn were now immortalized within the Point Reyes National Seashore. The fault line, however, was nothing but a subdued terrace just wide enough to allow two goats to safely pass. It cut cleanly across the rolling pasture where the alleged swallowing took place. I had come here to see what one geology textbook calls "the most famous geological fault in the world." There it was: a goat path. I knew there was more to the San Andreas than that. The same textbook told me that it rises like a wound out the Gulf of California, divides mountains and deep trenches, fractures farmlands and splits cities, then plunges below the Pacific Ocean, terminating as a giant submarine escarpment five kilometers high. From end to end, this gargantuan gash through the American southwest is a thousand kilometers long.

Everyone's heard about the San Andreas Fault. For hundreds of years it has inspired a multitude of popular songs, novels, theater productions, folklore and prophecies of doom. It is part of the mental furniture of anyone with even the slightest interest in geology. It ranks among the most intensively studied and monitored natural features on earth. When the San Andreas trembles, most of the world knows. But who ever hears about the faults of the northern Canadian Shield? They are equally gargantuan, and in my mind equally newsworthy though tremendously older. And they bear the scars of colossal earthquakes that could rival any that shake the San Andreas today.

The same kinds of forces that put Matilda in her grave slashed deep linear incisions across the rocks of the northern shield. When things get tense in the earth's crust, faulting offers an indispensable mechanism for stress relief. Faults occur wherever two opposing rock surfaces slip past each

Micro-fault on the McDonald mega-fault. Note the small linear veins of white quartz displaced by a few centimeters along the diagonal crosscutting fault. (PHOTO: JAMIE BASTEDO)

other along a fracture. You get an earthquake along this fracture when pent-up tensions are suddenly released and the rock surfaces snap into new geologically more comfortable positions. If there is a relative downward motion between rock faces, it's called a dip-slip fault. If movement is horizontal, with rock faces sideswiping each other, it's a strike-slip fault, alias wrench, transcurrent or tear fault—labels geologists apply to the San Andreas and to many of the major faults up north.

Faults express themselves in many ways. A single fault may build a front of mountains. Much smaller ones may create handholds for those that climb them. On the rolling bedrock plains of northern Canada, the telltale signs of faulting include prominent escarpments (which break what one geomorphologist calls the "reputed monotony of Shield scenery") and strings of finger-shaped lakes often beaded with long narrow islands. Along some faults you can follow this pattern for hundreds of kilometers.

The McDonald Fault is such a one. So prominent is its signature on the continent's crown that it can be well appreciated from outer space. Gazing upon northern Canada from the flight deck of an upside-down space shuttle, your eye is caught by a great sweeping lake shaped very much like a swan in flight: Great Slave Lake. It flies northeast on wings created by the lake's North Arm. Its extended neck and head lie along the East Arm, an oceanic "bay" 250 kilometers long. The East Arm owes its existence to the McDonald Fault, a strike-slip system that runs straight and true down its southern shore.

My first view of the McDonald Fault was through the window of an eastbound Twin Otter floatplane. Though the sky was cloudless that June morning, a gray-blue pall from distant forest fires hung over the East Arm. I asked the pilot if he could take us down to 150 meters "and just follow those cliffs." Those cliffs . . . We dropped out of the sky and fell into line with their rugged brows, then dropped some more. It then occurred to me that the pilot had brought us 150 meters from the water. That put the top of the cliffs about thirty meters *above us*. A tapestry of knife-edged sedimentary walls moved past my window. A few kilometers later the tapestry changed to knobby granite. Tiny pockets of tall white spruce clung to loose rubble at the base of the precipice. A peregrine falcon, flushed from its cliffside nest, flew in tandem with our plane for a few moments as if to drive us away.

"Look!" the passenger behind me suddenly exclaimed. "A monster lake trout!"

I peered straight down and saw nothing but gently breaking waves. "Whatever you say," I said, presuming wish fulfillment on his part.

Knifelike cliffs hundreds of meters high slice a clean line along the south shore of Great Slave Lake's East Arm. (PHOTO: JAMIE BASTEDO)

Indeed some of the world's most sought-after trout are down there, swimming around in one of the world's deepest lakes. Below the water surface, some of these cliffs drop another six hundred meters. I leaned hard against the glass, looking forward and aft, trying to comprehend the immense scale of the McDonald Fault. There was no end in sight. From our altitude, this grand escarpment ran off into the smoke from horizon to horizon. Our black and yellow Twin Otter was an insect buzzing alongside the handrails of the Queen Mary. The trim edge of this immense ship towered defiantly above the dark blue waters of the East Arm.

Our plane set down on a calm narrow bay in front of a palatial log cabin called Trophy Lodge. This is a fishing hide-away tucked into the outer limits of the East Arm near a place marked on the map as Reliance. There's really nothing to Reliance. No community I mean, unless you call this lodge, a couple cabins across the bay and an abandoned government weather station a community. A planeload of environmental bureaucrats, myself included, had come here precisely because this place was so out of the way, so far from phones, fax machines, deputy ministers and the like. We had retreated to this place of no distractions to bravely forge a conservation strategy for the entire circumpolar world. A big job, yes, but my boss felt somebody had to do it.

No distractions . . . sure. On our first morning all the lodge's windows were flung wide open. Try rolling up your sleeves and pounding out policies with sunlight streaming down on your work table like liquid honey and with the Christmasy scent of boreal sage tickling your nostrils. Try formulating strategic goals and objectives with a bald eagle cackling overhead, herring gulls laughing on the beach and a nearby yellow warbler declaring that you are so *sweet-sweet-sweet-you-are-so-sweet*. As the afternoon wore on, my colleagues swore that above the merry din outside, they could clearly hear something else calling their names. It was the lake trout. To my ears this sound was inaudible. What I heard calling me was the rocks.

The conservation strategy could wait. At three o'clock we closed our government reports, ate a final cheese croissant (freshly baked), then exploded out the lodge door like kids on the last day of school. Everyone piled into aluminum outboard boats. With fishing rods dangling over their bows, four boats took off around the point toward the "secret" bay where our guide had said the trout lay waiting. A fifth boat, carrying me alone, took off in the opposite direction, aimed directly at the highest cliffs in sight.

It was a brisk boat ride. Though heat waves shimmered off the dead calm lake surface, I was dressed to the nines in windproof thermal gear. An early morning swim, if you could call

A cave dweller's view of the East Arm's interior peninsulas. (Photo: Chris O'Brien)

it that, told me that the water had not risen much beyond the freezing point. Nor apparently had the air immediately above it. Less than a week ago thick pans of rotting candle ice choked the waters where my boat now sped.

The cliffs loomed nearer and higher. Some rose surgically straight out of the water. Great for sight-seeing, lousy for landing. I planed at half throttle just a few meters out from the shore. Farther on, the shoreline softened. But still there was no shelter to be had here—no bays, no inlets, just an unswerving cobble beach. I chose to land below a slight kink in the granite cliff, where I hoped the climbing would be easier.

Three hours of rock rambling along the crest of the McDonald Fault had thoroughly teased my sense of wonder. Supper could wait. Clearly something monumental had occurred here. The rocks along this part of the fault line were naked except for a few stalwart jack pines and a spattering of black and lime-colored lichens. On some exposures I discovered wide curtainlike swaths of twisted fractures. Intense shearing forces had created these patterns, tearing the crystalline bedrock as if it were so much burlap. Some of the larger fractures were filled with ground-up fragments of rock that geologists call cataclastics—rocks mashed to a pulp by cataclysmic mechanical stress. I saw long veins of white quartz, dark-speckled gabbro and purplish gray carbonate that had been ripped apart into steplike ribbons of rock. Elsewhere I saw vast rock gardens of laminated gneiss that showed weird Z-shaped folds seemingly raked into place by mischievous Zen monks.

I sat down on a big flat chunk of red mudstone near the cliff edge to collect my racing thoughts. For a while I tried unsuccessfully to imagine the kind of power that must have been let loose to fracture and tear and bend and pulverize

Fractured, fissured and faulted bedrock—lingering scars from ancient geological upheavals. (Photo: Jamie Bastedo)

rocks like this. I thought about how long it would take me to walk from one end of the McDonald Fault to the other. At a naturalist's pace three months should do me. In a pinch, two. Getting lost would certainly not be a problem. Who could miss it? I reflected on the pros and cons of making the East Arm into a national park—as some would have it.

"This is a spectacular landscape," says the official park proposal, "an immense archipelago of islands in Great Slave Lake, long fault-block escarpments, gorges, waterfalls, and much more." If it became a park, I wondered, would German tourists clad in wet suits some day jump off these cliffs and hang glide down to the islands hundreds of meters below me?

At this point my thought train collided with my hunger. I unzipped my pack and pulled out another croissant (slightly squished) and a thermos of cold lemonade (freshly squeezed). Like a basking lizard I sat on that boulder, soaking up the late afternoon sun, sipping lemonade, drinking in an eagle's view of a raw and lovely land. Reflection and refreshment up on the McDonald line. This is as big as wilderness gets, I thought, as I stood up and saluted the East Arm with wide-open arms. Then over the edge I went, by foot.

Before launching my boat from the shore, I paused to admire the delightful array of cobbles on the beach. They were all sedimentary rocks ferried to this spot during the most recent pass of glacial ice. Tiling much of the beach were platter-sized pans of flaky red shale that appeared stockpiled for backyard patio installation. I picked up a stately chunk of layered mudstone about the size of a bread loaf. It looked to me like a giant candy bar with thick reddish brown layers being the chocolate and pockets of lighter coarser material being the caramel filling. Another rock showed intricate pink and brown layers of sandstone that were sliced through in a perfect right angle by a vein of pearly white quartz. Many rocks displayed alternating grooves and ridges from one layer to the next, the classic sculpting action of differential erosion. Some rocks were burnished and round, having rolled from far away down ancient rivers or glacial meltwater streams. Others were coarse and angular, having fallen off nearby sedimentary cliffs or having been nosed here by a glacier from the islands just across the bay.

"There's some pretty strange rocks out there," veteran prospector Dave Smith told me back in town. Smith is a man of few words, Viking eyes and an astonishingly large beard. When not banging rocks Smith manages a shipping company called East Arm Freighting and skippers its one and only freighter, a small green and white tug called the *Hearne Channel*. Depending on the mood of the East Arm, it can take Smith anywhere from one to nine days to make the supply run from Yellowknife to Lutsel K'e, a tiny Chipewyan com-

Glacial flotsam and jetsam line the shore of the East Arm in the form of sedimentary mudstones, limestones and errant chunks of granite. (PHOTO: JAMIE BASTEDO)

munity west of Reliance. During one of these trips he discovered a thick band of carbon among sediments laid down long before there was much life around to create it. "It doesn't make much sense to find that stuff in rocks so old," Smith said.

He wasn't looking for carbon. He was looking for veins of

zinc, copper, nickel and of course gold, all of which are found on or near the McDonald Fault and none of which have yet proven worthy of mining. All prospectors know that the abundant fissures and fractures associated with fault zones provide a convenient pathway for mineral-rich broths that occasionally blast up through the earth's crust. The San Andreas Fault put scores of mines on the map of California. "Why not here?" asked Smith. He once got a "decent kick of gold" in a rock sample he chipped from the fault zone. But that was twenty years ago. "I've been too busy to go back there and check it out."

Mining limestone, of all things, has been one of the jobs keeping Smith so busy. His specialty is stromatolitic limestone that contains fossils of the oldest life-forms on earth. The rims of several islands in the East Arm are polka-dotted with large cell-like humps and blotches created by the proverbial slime that once ruled the planet. Our earliest ancestors took the form of mushroom-shaped microbial mats composed of colonies of blue-green algae or cyanobacteria, what *Scientific American* calls "the life form with the longest if not the most distinguished lineage on earth." In their heyday, from about 2 billion to 680 million years ago, these stromatolites formed huge reefs in shallow tide pools and sheltered lagoons along the margin of tropical seas.

Now beautifully preserved and on display beneath subarctic skies, these stromatolites have become a scientific commodity of special interest to the Japanese. A few summers back Smith received a rather large order from the Kanagawa Prefectural Museum of Natural History in Osaka. It needed thirty tons of stromatolites right away. He happily took the job and applied his well-honed drilling, cutting and blasting skills to carve some prime specimens out of the East Arm. Back at the museum Japanese paleontologists glued the care-

Beautifully preserved stromatolite fossils, remnants of the blue-green slime that ruled the planet two billion years ago. (Photo: Jamie Bastedo)

fully numbered fossils back together to create a mammoth twenty-meter high wall of stromatolites now beheld by millions each year and all supplied courtesy of East Arm Freighting.

Steve Goff is another man with an intimate knowledge of East Arm geology. A former Londoner with a flair for Celtic

Thick Precambrian sediments incised by a sensuous glacial groove.
(PHOTO: JAMIE BASTEDO)

music, Dr. Goff is a federal geologist who makes his base camp in Yellowknife. He earned a doctorate banging the sediments and volcanics that line the peninsulas and islands north of the fault line. "There's a hell of a lot of sediments down there, and when you measure them up across the East Arm, you find an enormous increase in thickness as you approach the McDonald Fault system." Goff explained how for hundreds of millions of years this massive linear feature cutting across the shield served as a geological rudder that piloted the flow of sediments into the East Arm. "That's a very profound structure out there," said Goff. "That fault goes right down to the mantle."

Now this intrigued me. Having scaled the McDonald Fault's lofty crown and pondered its awesome length, I hadn't thought much about how far *down* it reaches into the earth's crust.

There was only one man to turn to: deep geologist Alan

Jones, senior research scientist with the Geological Survey of Canada. Equipped with a string of geophysics degrees from Britain and instruments so sensitive they are considered restricted technology by the U.S. military, Dr. Jones makes regular voyages into the inner space of the North American continent. I asked him how he travels.

"There are basically two ways to understand deep structures beneath us," he said. "To look into the ground, you either use sound waves or electromagnetic waves." Geologists of the former school employ a kind of sonar device to see deep underground. They set off huge explosions or drive "dancing elephant trucks" over the land and translate the pattern of echoing sound waves into images corresponding to the rocks below. This technology takes you down to about fifty kilometers, not deep enough for Jones. He tunes into the electromagnetic response of rocks. "My instruments see conducting structures—not copper wires but all sorts of rocks, some more conducting than others," he told me. How far down can Jones see? "About one thousand kilometers is the best we can do," he admitted. Below that the magnetic field of the earth's core screws up the readings on his magnetometers. I asked Jones what personally motivates him to do this deeply probing work. As a response he quoted the words of Gene Rodenberry, creator of the ever popular series *Star Trek:* "To boldly go where no man has gone before!" Then he added, "I have a thirst for knowledge. This may sound trite, but I think that's what drives most scientists. We certainly don't do it for the money."

In 1996 Jones and a field assistant drove a truckload of magnetometers, cables, batteries, electrodes and other field instruments to Great Slave Lake. They kept driving as far as they could along the north shore until the road ended. Then they turned around and drove two hundred kilometers in the opposite direction at a snail's pace. Covering fifty sampling sites in total, they took electromagnetic pictures of basement rocks at depths ranging from a few meters to a few hundred kilometers underground. En route, their recording instruments were struck by lightning three times. They had to wait at one sampling site while a black bear sat on their recording box. "When the bear wandered off we rushed out and did the fastest data retrieval ever." At another site thieves walked off with a one-hundred dollar battery that powered their instruments, "but thank goodness," said Jones, "they left the twenty-five-thousand-dollar magnetometer." At yet another site somebody stole the wheel nuts off one of their trucks, a crime discovered only as they tried to drive away. But eventually they made it to the McDonald Fault, one of Jones's special target zones. They crossed it south of Great Slave Lake in a region where the fault is deeply buried under much younger Palaeozoic sediments, where it is invisible to ordinary earthlings. Jones of course had a good look at it. What he saw startled him.

"I saw a very strong effect in the data exactly at this point. My results told me that there is some very large conducting structure thirty to fifty kilometers below and exactly parallel to the fault zone." Jones had traveled to the very roots of the McDonald Fault, which lay roughly at the bottom of the earth's crust.

So there was much more to this ancient fault than those contorted and ruptured rocks I had seen up on the cliffs—or even the cliffs themselves. I gradually began to fathom in a visceral way what so many geologists and textbooks were telling me: These features were merely surface expressions of deep-seated scars created by continents in collision. Ironically it was my pilgrimage to a young and active fault zone, the San Andreas, that helped me to bring to life the inner workings of this long-ago collision.

First, imagine yourself standing directly on the San Andreas Fault back in the cow pasture at the Shafter Ranch. You are looking west along a fence line that runs perpendicular to the fault. In the space of less than five minutes the 1906 earthquake tore this fence apart, leaving two ragged ends offset by six meters. It was the end on your right that went for a ride. To geologists that makes it a right lateral strike-slip fault. The side that moved is on the Pacific Plate, which stretches west to Japan and south to New Zealand. This, the biggest thing on earth, is chugging to the northwest at around five centimeters per year. Behind you is the North American Plate carrying a load that includes 99 percent of our continent plus a healthy portion of the Atlantic sea floor. The sideswiping of these two geological behemoths creates what American geologist Stephen Harris calls "the most notorious earthquake zone on earth."

In *Agents of Chaos*, Harris muses on the future of the San Andreas Fault. He predicts that "the 1989 earthquake that toppled buildings, bridges and freeways from Santa Cruz to San Francisco was not the anticipated 'Big One.'" He views these events as "only local neighborhood dress rehearsals for the great devastation that will sweep through much larger sections of California in the near future." Local seismologists (of which there are many) have made meticulously detailed prophecies of what's in store for Californians. They measure expected death tolls in the tens of thousands, the number of homeless in the millions and the costs of property damage in the billions. They predict that the Big One will arrive most certainly within the next fifty years. And judging from the relative youthfulness of the San Andreas Fault (only thirty million years), they carry the story much further, predicting a long and lively future for movement down the line. Fifteen million years from now (a drop in the bucket of geological

time) Los Angeles, such as it may or may not be, will have
rafted far enough north to become a rather large western
suburb of San Francisco. In fifteen million years, they say, the
Giants and the Dodgers could be crosstown rivals.

Now imagine yourself back on that cliff edge where I
once sipped lemonade in the sun. At your feet is the
McDonald Fault. Shouldering the sediment piles that line the
East Arm and stretching seven hundred kilometers north to
the Arctic coast is the oldest piece of the planet, the Slave
geological province, parts of which are at least four billion
years old. At your back is a twenty-five-kilometer-wide belt
of rock that in the words of one local geologist has been
"fractured like crazy": the Great Slave Shear Zone. Behind
that is the largest of the Canadian Shield's seven major
provinces: the Churchill. It reaches east and south of the East
Arm clear to Baffin Island and Hudson Bay. The Slave and the
Churchill were once in motion, grinding past each other in
opposite directions along a mammoth fault plane that now
sutures them together.

At opposite ends of the geologic fabric called North
America are two profound rips that have much in common—one very young in California, one very old in the
Northwest Territories. Like the San Andreas, the McDonald
Fault is a right lateral strike-slip fault. The most useful bench-
marks for gauging direction of movement along fossil faults
are dikes—vertical, sheetlike intrusions of rock—that crosscut
the fault line and predate most of the sliding. As luck would
have it, several swarms of ancient dikes crisscross the
McDonald. From your cliff-top vantage point over the East
Arm, most of these dikes have been severed, then ferried to
your right—just like Shafter's fence line. Like the San Andreas
Fault, the McDonald is also a thousand kilometers long.
Beyond the East Arm a good portion of the fault is "topo-

graphically subdued," or buried altogether. Largely unnoticed it extends northeast way over to the Thelon Game Sanctuary and southwest almost as far as the Rocky Mountain Trench. Paralleling both the McDonald and San Andreas faults is a tangled network of secondary faults that branch out from the mother fault like fractures in thin ice behind a skater. Both the San Andreas and McDonald faults are sandwiched by a massive shear zone and thick sedimentary rocks. And the basement rocks lining both faults bear the scars and contusions of hundreds of earthquakes occurring over millions of years.

But unlike the San Andreas, up on the McDonald line, all is now and ever shall be quiet. Here the slipping and dipping is over. On this point Precambrian geologists seem to agree. "As far as I can make out," said rock banger Steve Goff, "that fault has seen its best days." Deep Earth inspector Alan Jones concurred. "That fault is locked in there solid. It's not going anywhere." The relatively recent plastering of North America's flanks by the Appalachians on one side and the Rocky Mountains on the other thoroughly put the brakes on any further jousting between geological provinces of the Canadian Shield, including the Slave and the Churchill. The future of the McDonald Fault therefore seems geologically secure. Both in the short and long term, the biggest jolts to shake it will likely come not from convulsions of magma down under but from underground detonations set off by miners disemboweling nearby rock for gold, diamonds and such. Unlike Los Angeles and San Francisco, Yellowknife and Baker Lake are not apparently destined to become closer neighbors.

"So," I asked Dr. Goff, "if this region is so stable, what can we expect to see in the vicinity of the McDonald Fault fifteen million years from now?" Goff said, "Well, it'll proba-

House-sized boulders of granite lazily give way to gravity along the McDonald Fault zone. (PHOTO: JAMIE BASTEDO)

bly look pretty much the same. Certainly the topography may change. Differential erosion never stops. And who knows how many glaciers might sweep through here during that time." I asked him about one of his favorite subjects: sediments. Could another marine transgression or new mountain chain again dump huge loads of sediments into the East Arm? "We can't expect the massive sediment loads that we got in the past," he said, "since we're dealing mostly with a rock plain. The lakes will very likely be gone. Geologically lakes and rivers are the most ephemeral entities going. But by and large, the area probably won't look a hell of a lot different even a *billion* years from now."

Stability. Come what may the sutures binding the northern Canadian Shield together will hold fast for the geologically foreseeable future. The McDonald Fault seems destined to heal. But what forces caused the faulting in the first place? What created this wound and kept it open and trembling off and on for millions of years? Precambrian geologists have debated this point to near ideological extremes. As beautifully exposed and well preserved as the rocks may be, they are indeed a confusing lot. The man who pioneered the first detailed field studies of the McDonald Fault in the 1960s, E. W. Reinhardt, observed that "all rocks have experienced a complex structural evolution much of which is difficult or impossible to decipher." Unfortunately neither Dr. Reinhardt nor anyone else was available to take field notes when all this happened. The only living witnesses to the most recent earthquakes along the McDonald Fault were the 2-billion-year-old stromatolites that Dave Smith chiseled out for the museum in Osaka.

Those geologists who are prone to dicker may breathe hot sulfurous fumes down my neck and anoint me with geyser water when I declare that the story may go *something* like this. It begins around 2.8 billion years ago back in the Archean Era, which literally means the earth's "most ancient time." By then a piece of real estate resembling the Slave province was a well-seasoned proto-continent unto itself, rafting around the planet pretty much on its own. Trundling at around five centimeters per year, as continental plates do today, it easily could have covered fifty thousand kilometers in a billion years. Then other proto-continents started popping their granite heads above the primeval seabeds of basalt. Among them was what is now the Slave province's western neighbor, the Bear, which emerged a few hundred million years later. That's when the banging began in earnest. According to geo-storyteller, Ron Redfern, "the early Archean proto-continents collided, amalgamated, and separated perhaps more vigorously and frequently in the tumultuous circumstances of the earth's formative years than they do in the comparative geologic calm of today." It seems that the Bear and the Slave likely amalgamated and traveled as one for a while. Then they came to rest over two mantle plumes, or stationary hot spots, much like the zone of crustal weakness that today delivers lava to the Hawaiian Islands, only much bigger. One of the hot spots was located in the region of the Coronation Gulf up on the Arctic coast. The other was located where the East Arm is today.

There were molten swellings in the basement. There was cracking in the crust. Gigantic fissures formed above each hot spot. One arm from each fissure zone joined in a continuous line along the suture that held the Bear and Slave together. The suture let go. One continent again became two. Seawater filled the growing gap. A midocean spreading ridge like today's Mid-Atlantic Ridge drove the Bear and the Slave over two thousand kilometers apart before the rifting stopped. Then for some unknown reason the movement of continents went into reverse. The Bear cruised down from what we now call the northwest, bound for a head-on collision with the Slave.

The extent of folding, faulting and flipping now visible where the ultimate impact occurred suggests that this reunion of continents was extremely violent. Upon collision the Bear thrust itself up and over the western margin of the

Slave along what geology maps call the Wopmay Fault Zone. Some geologists would call this a deformational event, others an orogeny. The more daring call it mountain building. By whatever name, this event was perhaps akin in power to the ramming of India into China. Look what's happening there: the Himalayas.

Like a string of fender benders in tight traffic, the Bear–Slave collision in turn sent the Slave crashing into the Churchill, putting a sizable dent into its northwest corner. The skidding along plate margins started in earnest around 2.2 billion years ago and finally came to a halt half a billion years later. This long drawn-out collision of the Slave and the Churchill added a distinctive signature to the northern Canadian Shield. Two huge strike-slip faults were scribed into the tablet of primeval bedrock. Along the Slave's eastern margin was the Bathurst Fault and to the south, the McDonald.

Reinhardt's pioneering studies along the McDonald Fault identified three major phases of movement. The first phase was mostly horizontal. That's what displaced some of those crosscutting dikes by eighty kilometers or more. The other two phases were mainly vertical. That's what caused the bottom to fall out of the East Arm. At some point during the shakedown, the crust below the rifted arms of the Great Slave hot spot collapsed. Geology textbooks often show this process by depicting a tidy block of rock dropping straight down between two parallel faults. They label it a *graben* fault, after the German word for grave. In the East Arm, things weren't quite so simple. "It's rather more like a semi-*graben*," according to Dr. Goff. The crust did drop cleanly along a well-defined fault plane lining the south shore of the East Arm, bestowing on us those spectacular north-facing cliffs. But along the opposite shore, where much less fracturing occurred, the crust warped downwards rather than dropped.

The net effect of this vertical displacement was the creation of a huge trough paralleling the McDonald Fault. Multiple passes of glaciers abutting the fault line were steered into the chasm. This repeated channeling of glacial power eventually scooped out a basin we now call Great Slave Lake.

Over hundreds of millions of years the East Arm trough also served as a favored channel for massive amounts of sediments. Fine silts, coarse boulders and just about everything in between found repose on the chasm floor. As the surrounding land shed myriad skins of rock kilometers thick, as oceans ebbed and flowed, as glaciers advanced and retreated, and as mountains rose and fell in distant terranes, the wheel of deposition, cementing and erosion rolled on unabated down the McDonald line.

All these comings and goings of earthly resources continued long after the McDonald Fault ground to a halt around 1.8 billion years ago, during the late Precambrian Era. It hasn't budged since, nor perhaps will it ever budge again. But regardless of hard-rock ideology, what properly constituted geologist could walk that line, peer over those celebrated cliffs and stroke those crazy rocks without dreaming about those long-ago days when it *was* in motion, say 2 billion years ago, when periodic jousting between the Slave and the Churchill plates was in full swing.

Like a sperm whale trying to surface below an anchored ship, a spasmodic lurch of magma bearing out of the northwest pounded into the pliable underbelly of the floating Slave proto-continent. Deep crustal tensions, pent up for decades, now became acute. On the surface, beneath greenish yellow skies and a tropical Precambrian sun, the land lay naked and still. Errant wisps of fine reddish dust played among the angular boulders and lava bombs that spattered the mudstone desert. Sporadic bursts of acrid steam escaped through small cracks in the brittle desert floor. Where the desert met the sea, there stood towering, knife-edged cliffs that exposed bizarrely skewed bands of sedimentary and volcanic rocks. Below the cliffs were rounded feet of granite bedrock that sloped steeply into the water, now stirred by the wind into gentle onshore swells. Dust and steam and waves. On the surface nothing else moved. But this ship was tugging at its moorings. Something had to give.

The giving began with a sharp snapping sound. Great blocks of bedrock hundreds of meters wide tore loose from their crystalline cradles. A low booming thunder accompanied the arrival of widespread tremors. For the first time in thirty years, the Slave was once again in motion. At first, movement along the fault was slow and feeble. Five seconds after the first tremors, the mudstone desert began rolling much like the sea waves below. Cracks splayed out from the fault line and raced across the surface. Some opened wide enough to admit loose boulders. New jets of steam were violently expelled from others. The principal shock came twenty seconds into the quake. Just below the desert surface, pockets of groundwater burst open, instantly liquefying the loose bone-dry sediments above. Outbursts of quicksand flew into the air. More thunderous booms. The cliffs reeled and slumped. Along a series of major fractures they dropped meters at a time in a steplike fashion, creating new tiers of wide seaside ledges. Huge sedimentary slabs of rock broke free and fell into the sea. An airborne slurry of pulverized rock and sand followed in their wake.

Five minutes later a severe aftershock shook the entire length and breadth of the fault zone. An undersea escarpment three kilometers high became dislodged at its roots. As it rocked toward a more balanced footing, it abruptly let go of a mountain's worth of sediments. A submarine landslide plummeted towards the sea bottom, which in turn pushed ahead of it a mountain's worth of water. The surface of the sea began to hiss as seething ribs of meter-high seismic waves took flight, accelerating to speeds exceeding eight hundred kilometers an hour. The waves sprinted low and fast over the open sea. In their path, just minutes away, was a sickle-shaped archipelago of volcanic islands surrounded by wide warm-water lagoons. As the waves approached, their unbridled energy became concentrated in the shallower waters, and they curled into giant frothing crests. Water was suddenly sucked away from the island margins, exposing a massive slimy carpet of bulbous stromatolites on the floor of the drained lagoons. When the waves finally slammed into the shore, they were eighteen meters high. The torrents of sediment liberated by this collision swept back into the sea, smothering billions of the earth's first citizens in a thick layer of fresh muck.

All this to move a continent forward ten meters in as many minutes.

Had the log palace called Trophy Lodge been around in those days it too might have been smothered in muck, swallowed by a wave or abruptly flattened by a giant sedimentary slab dislodged from the neighboring cliffs. But for now—meaning a few million years into the Cenozoic Era, eight thousand years into the Holocene Epoch, at the end of the second millennium A.D., just into the first flush of summer with a stable arctic high locked overhead—all was calm. Unmolested by natural disasters or office chitchat our tiny band of well-meaning bureaucrats remained sequestered in the wilderness for three straight days. We labored long and hard on that conservation strategy, ennobled by good intentions to serve the best interests of posterity, secure in our faith that we could somehow influence the fate of such magnificent northern treasures as the East Arm.

Our output was both prodigious (in terms of paper) and profound (in terms of aspirations). If enacted to the letter our strategy would help protect in perpetuity "the naturally occurring variety of living and non-living things" clear across the far northern hemisphere. Before we committed this charge to paper there was a brief discussion, mostly over coffee, as to exactly what we meant by "non-living things." The prevailing opinion included water and air and of course rocks. Though we prided ourselves on achieving consensus, to my mind the issue remained unresolved. But our time was up. The drone of an approaching Twin Otter sent us scrambling for our briefcases.

Reflecting on the gnarly grandeur of the McDonald Fault cliffs, again from the air, I temporarily warped back through geological time. All the fruits of our sincere labors at the lodge seemed now like so much dust and air: intangible, untenable, of no consequence whatsoever to the destiny of this land. Offering silent apologies to posterity, I concluded for the moment that our carefully crafted plans would never stick to these rocks. In time—in *their* time—the rocks would shake them off easily as a caribou, fresh from a river crossing, shakes off water. This epic saga in stone, begun when the world was new, would surely triumph over anything we humans might concoct, whether it be a national park, a string of hard-rock mines, or, as was predicted during the 1930's gold rush, a constellation of great cities rimming the East Arm shores.

The fathomless forces that created the McDonald Fault and ultimately control its destiny bring into sharp focus the ephemeral nature of life. They make a plaything of mortality: mine, our species *Homo sapiens* and for that matter *any* species, except perhaps for stromatolites whose multibillion-year lineage persists today in obscure pockets of the seas. But, as Albert Einstein once said, it's all relative. I find a sense of comfort, even camaraderie when regarding such time-worn rocks in light of their own mortality. Like us, their inner anatomy pulsates with invisible energies. Their crystalline skin vents and collects atmospheric gases in a rhythmic sequence of prolonged breaths. Their frames grow and decay over successive generations as dictated by the eternal cycling of matter and nutrients. All these vital functions, akin to if not synonymous with life itself, stream through these ancient rocks, though at a much more relaxed pace than we are used to. When I behold the McDonald Fault in this way, the nagging challenge of bringing my puny existence into proper alignment with the abyss of earthly time seems less irksome. Maybe some day I'll meet this challenge head-on by taking that long walk down the McDonald line. Therein may lie my real business with these rocks.

EPILOGUE
MAKING CONTACT

*Each time I journey into the wilds of this great land,
I feel a sense of reconnection to the earth. . . . It is a
journey of adventure, discovery and spiritual connection to the wild and stunningly beautiful subarctic.*
—Leslie Leong, Our Forgotten North

It was Deutschland Day in the bush. By sheer coincidence four out of six of the tourists walking with me down the trail were German nationals. That sunny afternoon in late July the woods rang out with boisterous laughter and crisp Teutonic banter as these four birds-of-a-feather got to know each other in an alien land I did my best to show them. Occasionally when I wanted to get their attention, I would break in with a few exaggerated nods and repeat, "*Genau, genau!*" which more or less means "Exactly. Right on!" and the foreign foursome would gather round me with amused concentration.

There was Karin, a blond and blue-eyed ecologist with an earnest face and most inquiring mind. Last winter she sent me a thick "overview" of her postdoctoral research all the way from Bremen Universitåt. It proclaimed that Karin was going to "analyze and evaluate the reactions of northern boreal forest ecosystems to man-made stresses from mining and connected activities." Now, months later, here she was beside me, looking for a juicy bog to dig up.

"It was difficult to get financial support for my research proposal," she told me as we squished our way along the edge of a horsetail marsh. "There are very few people in Germany interested in boreal ecosystems." Not so for her lanky friend, Bettina. Back at the Universität she had spent the winter quietly steeped in her professor's passion for the North and now joined Karin as her trusted field assistant.

Then there were Werner and Wolfgang. When I first discovered their names on my tour list, my young girls and I spent some time developing our Bavarian accents, emphasizing between giggles, the slurred V as best we could. Verner and Volfgang. We found a certain rhythmic appeal in repeating their names. It turned out that neither one of them was from Bavaria, but that didn't stop them from making numerous good-natured wisecracks about northern hospitality.

"Ees there a beer garden up ahead?" they would ask me, laughing again as we penetrated farther into the forest. A solidly built man of seventy-three, Werner was big in most of his dimensions including his heart, I was to discover. Above his ruddy face and cropped bone-white hair he wore a navy blue sailor's cap that looked like it had been parked up there for a very long time.

"I am his baby cousin," announced Wolfgang, who looked to be in his midsixties. He was a smaller stouter man but equally ruddy.

My sole anglophone guests were Keeran and Patti, a married pair of well-seasoned birders from Vancouver. Keeran, with the sun-bleached Tilley hat and thick graying moustache, was also a professor. His specialty was not ecology but aboriginal myths and folklore. Between bird sightings and random bug attacks, I asked him if the landscape we were sauntering over brought any folktales to mind.

"As a matter of fact, it does," he said. Then he explained how mosquitoes were created after Raven ruthlessly chopped up his pesky mother-in-law into millions of itsy-bitsy pieces.

Along the trail our colorful crew picked raspberries, bear-berries and cloudberries and ate them right on the spot. Holding up a glistening orange cloudberry, I said, "You know, the Scandinavians make a wonderful liqueur out of these."

Wolfgang nodded. "I *must* have tried it," he said emphatically while reaching out to sample my berry.

Through the lens of a high-powered spotting scope, we hunted down and captured a distant pair of majestic Pacific loons loafing on a watery film of sunlight. We listened to the mew gulls mewing and the arctic terns rattling as these arch rivals jostled each other for perch spots on a tiny shoal of rock.

"Look! There are the young ones," cried Karin, pointing to a company of two-legged fluff balls retreating into the water. We stopped to a smell some cold soggy peat, for me the quintessential odor of all that is boreal.

"Just like the peat moss we buy for our gardens?" asked Patti.

"Exactly," I said, "only fresher." We all got down on our hands and knees to stroke a naked exposure of Precambrian lava rock burnished satin smooth by multiple passes of a continental ice sheet

"It is very old, yes?" asked Werner.

"Very," I said. I had seen, heard, touched, smelled and tasted it all before—perhaps a hundred times down this trail alone. But at one point in our journey, when suddenly struck giddy by the natural splendor around us, I had to declare quite frankly, "This place is intoxicatingly beautiful!"

At a pronounced crook in the trail, I had people look back over their shoulders to observe one of my favorite vistas on the subarctic. "Postcard pretty," said a tourist on a previous walk as she looked out at the shimmering lake through a natural frame of gently swaying cattails, nodding pink fireweed and stately white spruce. I told them about the homemade postcard I received from a globetrotting American family who once stood on this very spot.

"They asked me to take their picture right here with this lake in the background," I said. "Seven months later I got a Christmas card from them. Of all the pictures they might have taken in their travels they chose that particular one to mass-produce and send around to all their friends and family at Christmas." The photo showed a beaming family of four very much at home and at peace in the subarctic wilds. Beside it was the card's chosen message printed in swirly red letters: "Joy to the World."

"Ven I travel, I only send postcards to one person," said Werner, who then waited for me to ask, "And who might that be?" He pulled up his sweaty blue golf shirt to reveal a long wide scar that ran skunklike from the top of his rib cage clear to the bottom. "To my heart surgeon," he said proudly. I think I let out an audible gasp. "Thanks to him," Werner went on, "I am here with you today." Thanks to two major rounds of open-heart surgery, I learned, the last of which was a quadruple aortal bypass. Upon recovering from this news I reflexively reached behind me to feel for a lump in my backpack where my wilderness first-aid kit should be. The lump was there. What little good it might do me in a fix was not something I cared to think about.

Werner puffed down the trail ahead of us. "The bog I promised you is just around the corner," I called over my shoulder to Karin.

"Vunderful," she said.

We filed past Keeran who had suddenly stopped dead in his tracks. His binoculars were, as usual, clamped tightly against his eye sockets. "It looks to me like a greater . . . no it's a lesser yellowlegs."

"That would make sense," I said of the northern forest's most common shorebirds.

"What doesn't make sense," said Keeran, "is that this *shore-bird* is perched on the very top of that spruce tree."

Everyone else stopped abruptly to watch the teetering bird.

"You have to expect the unexpected up here," I told him. The bird teetered forward on its gangly legs, stuck out its skinny gray neck, then accosted us with a barrage of plaintive *tew-tew-tew*s. It launched repeated aerial forays at us when we stopped to have a good look at the bog—a so-called raised bog with a good bounce to it.

"It is most springy," said Wolfgang as he tried a few enthusiastic hops.

The bog was stuffed through and through with peat, that marvelous mire made from undecomposed plant matter. I scooped out a handful and examined the stringy reddish brown moss.

"Most of this is *Sphagnum* moss," I said. "It grows in very soggy, acidic conditions where there's little oxygen. Bacteria hate this. Nothing breaks down. This moss has probably been piling up here for centuries." I passed the sample around. "It's incredibly absorbent, perfect for dressing wounds or lining a baby's bottom. A good thermal insulator too. You can chink your log cabin with it." I pointed to the ground. "And you can bet it's mighty cold down there even on a hot day like this."

Karin dropped to her knees. "How deep down is the permafrost, do you think?" she asked me.

I pulled a plastic orange toiletry shovel out of my pack. "Let's find out," I said.

Karin, Bettina and I took turns probing the peat, digging through decades of history with each shovelful. Keeran and

Patti remained riveted on the yellowlegs, which continued to hurl abuse at us all. Wolfgang seemed to be watching the clouds. I looked up from our work to see a procession of wind-shorn clouds hovering probably a dozen kilometers above our heads.

Clunk. "Vee must have hit it," said Karin, smiling widely as she pulled the shovel and her peat-encrusted arm out of the hole.

I stuck my arm in as far as it would go. My fingertips made contact with an ice-cold table of frozen peat. "Real live discontinuous permafrost!" I announced. "One of the classic signatures of the subarctic." Even the birders came over for a look. And Wolfgang too. But where was Werner? In the excitement I had forgotten to keep close tabs on him.

My stomach turned to ice as I looked up and down the trail for a tall wide man in a sailor's cap. Had he fallen in the lake? Had the warranty run out on his surgeon's parts and services?

"Aha!" said Werner's younger cousin and self-proclaimed guardian. "There he ees." Wolfgang was pointing to a large whale-shaped outcrop of rock that rose steeply from the bog's far edge. On the back of the whale was a large figure hunched over on all fours as if in solemn prayer—or in extreme pain. His bowed head was hanging just a few centimeters above the rock surface and his body was deathly still. I grabbed my pack and sprang over the bog's hummocky surface towards Werner.

I was relieved to see his arm fling out toward me as I drew near. Without taking his eyes off the rock, Werner was beckoning me to look at something. Then he sat up straight and pointed at a spot just in front of his bent knees. "They don't seem very interested in my candy," he said.

"Who, Werner?" I asked, still a little shaken.

"Those ants!" he exclaimed. "Never in my life have I seen such big black ants!"

The whole time we were digging up the peat bog, Werner had been over here communing with the ants, studying their movements and offering them chewed up pieces of peppermint candy. We watched them silently for a while longer as they streamed in single file across the warm rock. Then he suddenly stood up and stretched from head to toe, producing an audible crack that came from somewhere along his large frame. With his hands propped firmly on his hips, he turned to address the yellowlegs now perched on a fire-scarred snag just a few meters away. The bird's relentless bobbing and screaming seemed directed squarely at Werner, an insult he countered with a big-hearted belly laugh.

On the way back to the road—and to civilization—our mood was temporarily spoiled by a couple of teenage boys going in the opposite direction down the trail. They each carried a fishing rod, a six-pack of beer and a very large machete knife. They each wore a spanking new bug jacket, high-top basketball shoes and no pack. So much for the beer cans, I thought. I'll be picking them off the trail on my next tour since these guys have no way to pack out their empties. And what's with those knives? Why would anyone carry a huge machete down a trail dominated by widely spaced jack pine and bald-face bedrock? The boys passed us without a nod or a word. But their faces betrayed a puzzled mix of both mischief and guilt. A few steps ahead we discovered the reason for the knives and the faces. Just about every birch and aspen tree beside the trail with a diameter of a few centimeters or less had been cleanly, efficiently and mindlessly hacked down.

"Where does this kind of thing fit into your list of human impacts on the boreal forest?" I asked Karin rhetorically. She gave a quick shrug in reply. I spent much of the last leg of the hike silently brooding over the prospects of safeguarding the subarctic against such disrespect. From oil spills and toxic mine emissions to petty vandalism and littering, these environmental misdemeanors regularly shatter my chronic delusion that a wilderness this big can find safety in its sheer size alone.

After all the usual handshaking and fond farewells back in town, our ephemeral troupe of hikers dispersed to various corners of the globe, never to meet again. As for me, I went straight to my home-based office to look up what little file material I had on ants. I found one obscure article entitled "Life Histories of Subarctic Ants" written by a myrmecologist, an ant scientist, from none other than Germany. It was my turn to let go a belly laugh. A certain Dr. Heinze begins his article with the assertion that "The ant fauna of boreal and alpine biomes consists of a monotonously small number of species and thus has been given little attention." Hah! I thought. Tell that to my friend Werner. Never had I seen a man pay so much attention to ants. This burly Berliner addressed the lowliest of beings with the kind of affection and wonder that I might have expected from a child many decades younger.

Werner's door on the subarctic opened upon its ants. For Karin and Bettina it was its permafrost and peat. For Wolfgang it was berries and clouds. For Patti I sensed it was rocks. For Keeran it most definitely was birds. On countless tours through many years, I have watched this land work similar magic on people from all over the world. I'm guessing that it's the same story for all visitors and residents alike. For those who are willing to genuinely slow down and take the time to befriend the landscape, it *will* open up. The subarctic will show itself to you through one of its infinite portals, one that resonates uniquely with you. Your door to the subarctic might open upon its snow, flowers or northern lights; berries, birds or, yes, even bugs. Reach through that door and the land will reach back to you, beckoning you toward greater intimacy. You may well discover that the distances you travel and the ground that you tread are as much within you as without.

BIBLIOGRAPHY

EPIGRAPH
Wolfe, L.M. *Son of the Wilderness: The Life of John Muir.*
Madison: University of Wisconsin Press, 1945

INTRODUCTION: REACHING NORTH
Lopez, B. *Arctic Dreams.* New York: Bantam, 1987.

KATSUNORI'S CALLING
The Northern Lights. Dir. A. Booth. Yellowknife Films and
the National Film Board, 1992.
Davis, N. *The Aurora Watcher's Handbook.* Fairbanks:
University of Alaska Press, 1992.
Ferber, P. ed. *Mountaineering: The Freedom of the Hills.*
Seattle: The Mountaineers, 1960.
Savage, C. *The Mysterious Northern Lights.* Vancouver:
Douglas & McIntyre, 1994.

SNOW SAGA
Bentley, W.A. and W.J. Humpheys. *Snow Crystals.* New
York: Dover Publications, 1962.

LaChapelle, E.R. *A Field Guide to Snow Crystals.* Vancouver: J.J. Douglas, 1969.

O'Neill, D. *The Firecracker Boys.* New York: St. Martin's Press, 1994.

Pruitt, W.O. *Wild Harmony: The Cycle of Life in the Northern Forest.* Saskatoon: Western Producer Prairie Books, 1983.

Sadler, D. *Winter: A Natural History.* Peterborough, Ontario: Broadview Press, 1990.

Wiliams, T.T. and T. Major. *The Secret Language of Snow.* San Francisco: Sierra Club/Pantheon Books, 1984.

LIVING DOWN UNDER

Banfield, A.W.F. *The Mammals of Canada.* Toronto: University of Toronto Press, 1974.

Dyck, A.P. and R.A. MacArthur. "Seasonal Variation in the Microclimate and Gas Composting of Beaver Lodges in a Boreal Environment." *Journal of Mammalogy* 74(1) (1993): 180-88.

Dyck, A.P. and R.A. MacArthur. "Daily Energy Requirements of Beaver in a Simulated Winter Microhabitats." *Canadian Journal of Zoology* 71(10) (1993): 2131-35.

Dyck, A.P. and R.A. MacArthur. "Seasonal Patterns of Body Temperature and Activity in Free-Ranging Beaver *(Castor canadensis)*." *Canadian Journal of Zoology* 70(9) (1992): 1668-72.

Hilfiker, E.L. *Beavers: Water, Wildlife and History.* Interlaken, New York: Windswept Press, 1991.

Ontario Ministry of Natural Resources. Novak, M., et al. *Wild Furbearer Management and Conservation in North America.* Toronto: Ministry of Natural Resources, 1987.

DASHING THROUGH THE SNOW

Cinq-Mars, J. and C.A. Martijn. "History of Archeological Research in the Subarctic Shield and Mackenzie Valley." *Handbook of North American Indians*, Ed. J. Helm. Washington: Smithsonian Institute, 1981. 30-39.

Nelson, R.K. *Make Prayers to the Raven: A Koyukon View of the Northern Forest.* Chicago: University of Chicago Press, 1983.

Northwest Territories. Department of Education, Culture and Communications. *Ernie's Earth: The Wonders of Winter.* Dir. R. Burnet. Yellowknife: Government of the Northwest Territories. Two-part video, 1994 and 1997.

Osgood, W. and L. Hurley. *The Snowshoe Book.* Brattleboro, Vermont: Stephen Greene Press, 1983.

Prater, G. *Snowshoeing.* Seattle: The Mountaineers, 1988.

PIKE PASSIONS

Jackman, P. "The Lunacy Report." *Globe & Mail* 6 July 1996.

Freshwater Fishes of Canada. Ottawa: Fisheries Research Board of Canada, Bulletin No. 184, 1979.

Sternberg, D. *Northern Pike and Muskie.* New York: Cy Decosse, 1992.

Wooding, F.H. *Lake, River and Sea-Run Fishes of Canada.* Madeira Park, B.C.: Harbour Publishing, 1994.

THE ABCs OF BUG PROTECTION

Bastedo, J. *Shield Country: Life and Times of the Oldest Piece of the Planet.* Calgary: The Arctic Institute of North America, 1994.

Bates, M. *The Natural History of Mosquitoes.* New York: Harper and Row, 1970.

Orwell, G. *Nineteen Eighty-Four.* London: Penguin Books, 1949.

Schneider, D. "Biter's Banquet." *Canadian Geographic.* May/June 1995: 52-57.

LIFE AT THE EDGE

Brown, Tom. *Tom Brown's Field Guide to Nature and Survival for Children.* New York: Berkley Books, 1989.

Johnson D., et al. *Plants of the Western Boreal Forest and Aspen Parkland.* Edmonton: Lone Pine, 1995.

Hotchkiss, N. *Common Marsh, Underwater and Floating-Leaved Plants of the United States and Canada.* New York: Dover Publications, 1972.

Lamoureux, G. *Plantes Sauvages des Lacs, Rivieres et Tourbieres (Wild Plants of Lakes, Rivers and Peat Bogs).* Saint-Augustin, Portneuf, Quebec: Fleurbac, 1987.

Schofield, J.J. *Discovering Wild Plants: Alaska, Western Canada, the Northwest.* Anchorage: Alaska Northwest Books, 1989.

Walker, M. *Harvesting the Northern Wild.* Yellowknife: Outcrop Ltd., 1984.

FOOTPRINT OF FIRE

Hunt, A.J. *Fire and Northern Ecosystems: An Appraisal of Natural and Man Made Fires in the Western Arctic and their Effects on the Environment.* Winnipeg, MB: Environment Protection Board, 1973.

Janzen, S.S. "The Burning North: A History of Fire and Fire Protection in the Northwest Territories." MA Thesis, University of Alberta, 1990.

Kelsall, J.P., E.S. Telfer, and T.D. Wright. *The Effects of Fire on the Ecology of the Boreal Forest.* Ottawa: Canadian Wildlife Service, Occasional Paper No. 32, 1977.

Lewis, H.T. "Maskuta: The Ecology of Indian Fires in Northern Alberta." *Western Canadian Journal of Anthropology* 7 (1977): 15-52.

Lewis, H.T. and T. Ferguson. "Yards, Corridors and Mosaics: How to Burn a Boreal Forest." *Human Ecology* 16 (1) (1988): 57-77.

BETWEEN A ROCK AND A HARD PLACE

Bastedo, J. *Shield Country: Life and Times of the Oldest Piece of the Planet.* Calgary: The Arctic Institute of North America, 1994.

Hanmer, S. *Geology, Great Slave Lake Shear Zone, District of Mackenzie, Northwest Territories.* Ottawa: Geological Survey of Canada, Map 1740A, scale 1:50,000, 1991.

Hanmer, S. "Initiation of Cataclastic Flow in the Mylonite Zone." *Journal of Structural Geology* 11(6) (1989): 751-62.

Harris, S.L. *Agents of Chaos.* Missoula: Mountain Press, 1990.

Redfern, R. *The Making of a Continent.* New York: Times Books, 1983.

Reindhardt, E.W. *Geology of the Precambrian Rocks of Thunbun Lakes Map Area in Relationship to the McDonald Fault System, District of Mackenzie.* Ottawa: Geological Survey of Canada (1969): Paper 69-21.

Ritts, B.D. *The Sedimentology and Provenance of the Et-Then Group as a Record of Deformation on the McDonald Fault Zone, East Arm, Great Slave Lake, Northwest Territories.* Ottawa: Geological Survey of Canada, Current Research 1994-C (1994): 39-48.

Sibson, R.H. "Fault Rocks and Fault Mechanism." *Journal of the Geological Society of London* 133 (1979): 191-213.

ABOUT THE AUTHOR

JAMIE BASTEDO has a Master of Arts in Regional Planning and Resource Development from the University of Waterloo. He has lived and worked in the North for more than fifteen years. For several of those years he has been the popular host of CBC Radio's Northern Nature series, broadcast live and always outdoors from Canada's subarctic environs. In 1990 Jamie Bastedo launched CYGNUS Environmental Consulting, which specializes in environmental planning, assessment, education and eco-tourism. His previous books include *Blue Lake and Rocky Shore* and *Shield Country: Life and Times of the Oldest Piece of the Planet*. Jamie Bastedo lives in Yellowknife with his wife and two daughters.